# A Visual Narrative Concerning Curriculum, Girls, Photography Etc.

by

Hedy Emeline Fynebuik Bach

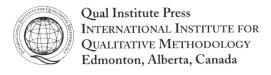

Qual Institute Press
INTERNATIONAL INSTITUTE FOR
QUALITATIVE METHODOLOGY
Edmonton, Alberta, Canada

*For information:*

Qual Institute Press
INTERNATIONAL INSTITUTE FOR
QUALITATIVE METHODOLOGY
Sixth Floor
University Extension Centre
8303–112th Street
University of Alberta
Edmonton, Alberta, Canada  T6G 2T4
Phone:    1-403-492-9041
Fax:        1-403-492-9040
Email: qualitative.institute@ualberta.ca
Or order books from our website: http://www.ualberta.ca/~iiqm/

Printed in Canada

*Canadian Cataloging-in-Publication Data*

Bach, Hedy, 1959–
        A visual narrative concerning curriculum, girls, photography etc
        Includes bibliographical references and indexes.
        ISBN 0-9683044-4-3
        1. Women—Education. 2. Education–Curricula.
        I. Title.
        LB2326.3.B33 1998            375'.00082            C98-900182-2

| | |
|---|---|
| Editor: | Janice M. Morse |
| Managing Editor: | Don Wells |
| Graphic Design: | Murray Pearson |
| Front Cover Artwork: | Hedy Bach |
| Back Cover Photo | Quinn Covington |

# CONTENTS

# DEDICATION

To Chloé, who is always looking.

# Acknowledgements

to show and express my gratitude
i recognize

my domestic backdrop as a valuable intellectual script

    Steve for always believing in me and reminding me what matters in the
intensity of joy and pain
    Chloé for pressing me to look when there is so much to see

my grrls

    beth for trust and tori
    maeve for coming into my life
    morgan for keeping me on my edge
    thya for risk and adventure
    you exceeded all my expectations by sharing yourselves with pleasure and
possibility

my colleagues for a community of caring people

    Jean for always seeing potential when I am blind
    Joy-Ruth for tremendous time and looking again and again
    Andrea for living "politics of the small"

Beth for sharp insight and space to wander
Ronna for sharing my passion for seeing
Julia for my search to find urban green space
Celia for her arms' length and space for rawness
Merle for reflective and fun friendship
Myer for remembering, always
Jan for patience in editing my work
Janice for listening deeply
Karen for living her words
Annie for responding
Chuck—well—wink wink
Ji-Sook for sharing herself
 for friends who live and have lived in the Centre for Research for
   Teacher Education and Development and the people who
    come to listen and look

the rest of our family
 and SPRINT
Karen for being there, always
Mom for understanding and generous gifts
Dad for what is in your heart
Truss for writing telling telling stories
Betty for her invisible work
Frank for always accepting
Mike and Leesa for helpful and caring connections

my technical support
 Sue in Grad Studies for listening
 ITC in Education for all their help

my financial support
 Alberta Heritage Scholarships
 Izzak Walton Killiam Memorial Scholarship

my graduate experience at the University of Alberta
 and the many people who have given generously of their time, patience, and
support to make this book possible

        and then some Mary-Janet!
and Don for helping this book emerge from the original dissertation.

# Preface

In this research, *A visual narrative: concerning curriculum, girls, photography etc.*, I deliberately explored the evaded as an intentional site concerning girls and curriculum. Le Dœuff (1991) writes, "There is no thinking which does not wander, and any serious work should have etc. in its title and honestly state that it will not stick to the topic" (p. xii). Her words invite my thinking to wander, which influences how I see my research questions and writing. I wrote my dissertation, which forms the basis for this book, as an orchestration of words and photography awake to celebrating my thinking positioned with the gaps, possibilities, and the etc. Researching self in relation with the girls' lived experiences frames my inquiry, and together we looked at issues that matter to us. My hope has been to invite rereadings and possibility for a discourse of the evaded in the lives of girls and women. Seeing and saying what matters to girls and the evaded curriculum require discussions of many other issues. For me, working with Maeve, Beth, Morgan and Thya helps me understand my story of high school and becoming a woman differently. Telling and retelling my stories in relation with the girls pressed me to look at the fine line between the personal and public of lived experience in my research. Listening closely to the girls' stories and seeing their photographs has "transformed [my] our intellectual work" (Clandinin & Connelly, 1994; Fine, 1994a). As a way to signify our lived experiences through my 4 years of doctoral research, I have composed a research text with photography and story as my way of coming to know self in relation to and being with girls. My narrative knowing is generated from our experiences and understanding of the body as a site of meaning-making. Trying to understand the working body and its connections outside-in and inside-out...to allow us to dig into our interior lives, providing an holistic approach that both connects and ruptures the fine line between body mind. (Bach, Kennedy, & Mickelson, 1997, p. 1)

I have written the research text in three notebooks as a way to document my learning as a graduate student of curriculum. Following Lessing (1962), Rich (1979), Le Dœuff (1991), and Calkins (1991), I borrowed the idea of a notebook genre. For me, notebooks enliven my desire for an image-laden book that originates with my interest in the visual arts and in underground 'zines:

Through a creative use of image and text, 'zines are perhaps the best cultural example of an intense interaction between projection and portrayal. Producing a 'zine is a search for a voice in response to feeling jettisoned and underrepresented in the mainstream press. 'Zines inject the personal into the public. (Gunderloy & Janice, 1992, p. 28)

Writing and positioning myself opens questions of legitimation, and along with Cixous (1994), I question who I am as I write this research text:

I wonder: when writing, am I transgressing? At first: no answer. Then: why am I asking myself if I am transgressing? If I were transgressing I would know, wouldn't I? I do not know....I am in uncertain incertitude. Sometimes I believe that I believe I am transgressing without knowing it, no trangressively. And sometimes I think: everything is transgression. And also; nothing is transgression. Am I transgressing by writing what I am writing? Or by not writing what I am not writing? Or both? (p. 97)

Injecting the personal into the public presses me to look at what Cixous (1994) asks: whose name and from what theoretical standpoint are they speaking; and who is their master, and where they are coming from? How I respond shapes the writing of my research text. I have questioned the construction of my self in the text and how I did the work by reflecting my self out. I see "personal experience methods" (Clandinin & Connelly, 1994) as a way to maintain an aura of intimacy and friendship, a sense of familiarity, in making the private public. In my writing I attempted to navigate a course that challenges and expands the identities of girls and myself as a teacher educator. I continue to see and hear concealed stories that are miseducative for girls. I see my stories composed over time as a way to inscribe reflexivity on my body, so I learn to write to what I do not understand. I imagine different futures for girls as they learn to negotiate tensions and contradictions among: the tortuous routes through debates about biology as destiny; the social construction of gender; economic parity; the authority of the phallocentric order; the myth of motherhood; the childcare debate; the body; class structure; race issues; the split between theory and practice; the beauty myth; the research on girls; the discourse on violence; and the etc.

I see how close I am and how I am seen with the girls. I represent my knowing and my shifting subjectivities of identity as I question my position and disrupt the acts of switching between observer and participant. Bringing my "peculiarities of inner experience" (Krieger, 1991) to the sites of struggle within my research experience does not relieve me of the necessity of critique of my position, my assumptions. Positioning of the author may be read as a prescriptive disclaimer, warning off critical interrogation (Alcoff, 1991). Can critique occur with an author who up front states they are speaking from a specified limited location? Is the need to position related to privilege? My notebooks acknowledge present theorists, educational researchers, fiction writers, songwriters, activists, poets, and visual artists whose works trouble an already interpreted world and turn the lens upon themselves. My hope has been to mess up the master's house, knowing "the master's tools will never dismantle the master's house" (Lorde, 1984 , p. 112).

    warning     warning     warning
              we're in the master's house
                  but not using the master's tools


    making strict observance necessary when you open this book

        you will need a lens ground with precision
              as you live with us
                  by
                      looking  closely  and  lingering  over  the
                          photographs
                  by
                      listening deeply to our conversations
                  have faith
                      you can dive into the seemingly unfathomable
                              and plumb its depths


        find your own questions in our stories
                      in the white spaces of the evaded

# Notebook 1

Irecognize something when looking in a mirror. I think about the other mirror, the one set opposite, in front and beside that creates infinite vision, as reflections reflect one another. What mirrors are set by their hands or by some body else's? I ask how I function when so many mirror handlers and so many reflections are simultaneously apparent.

I felt that to locate self within the research I needed to turn the lens on self. I show my cameraworks from a workshop on Phototherapy with Judy Weiser. In writing "eyes wide shut" I document a reflexive photographic look at my lived experiences of being a female researcher. I ask who am I in the research? I question who I learn from? Part of my answer is in how I view discomfort in my body, separating self from my reflections but acknowledging that these reflections inform the creation of my identity. I reinvent myself through experiences that have been multiplied, ruptured, enveloped, expanded and lost: "Telling you is the most minor attempt at loyalty, it is the most elementary form of candor. But can I not suspect in confession a hope for absolution" (Cixous, 1994, p. 97).

As a girl I grew up believing that "seeing is learning." I was certain that uncovering my desires would be accomplished only through agonizing female effort and that I would earn it through feminine chores. Was this a fallout from my training as a Judeo-Christian to be a "good girl?" As a good girl I searched for a middle ground for my sins, for the sins of others and for those I would never commit. It was a masochistic contract, a disruption, resulting in fiery images, rage, drugs, and crucifying my body.

I have inherited parts of this body and left parts behind. I am tied to my biography. I adopted sections of the glossy magazines that I read and carved out a self that clings to its cover story of being surveyor and surveyed. This "it" is me, no separation, no closure, not yet. Though I inherited a dual desire to be impenetrable and permeable, sealed and expanding I see a terrain of endless desert space. Even today, my identity is in a state of flux, my senses always alert, awkwardly poised, and exposed. I have continued to learn to live with these contradictory illusions.

no body said it would be simple

is this work?

i'm in the kitchen
writing on my lap top
i stare out of the window
a strange fog obscures the horizon
i have no excuse not to write
yet i feel
tied
by apron strings

seeing 'dust gorillas'
dog, cat and human hair
vacuum/wash/fold
laundry piled miles high
run the dishwasher
oh don't Ya forget to
write
this is work
isn't it?

two of "my" girls are coming over
for coffee
i want to be cheery
live the cover story
even when i feel down
i'm troubled by the scripts i trouble
the theories, telling telling stories
i read, talk and value
as i compete to balance

feeling overwhelmed

thinking

i see the women
in my community
looking tired
overloaded
ill
talking of battles
and going to war
finding the energy
to tackle
is this work?

what do i see for myself?

where is the meaning of life
love
what is a writing life?
being able to be alone
reflect on my lived experiences
the oxymoron
of the living life
this work

there are times when
i can laugh
at this work
other times i
cry
for the
women's work in the academy

where is my work?
where to begin
end
finish writing
the dissertation
the book
the novel

this is work
i like this work
but

wonder about the place
of women
professors'
graduate students'
work
in teaching and research
what are we keeping
what are we losing
what are we changing
what's in this work?
this
drudgery
grind
toil
exertion

this work
often unpaid
is
labor
an enterprise
a profession
an accomplishment
that is work
work
work for what?

caught in the
crossfire
stuck between what i do and what i ought to do
like
the bird in the cage
wanting to get out
be free
from the bars that seemingly hold me

## A POSITION NARRATIVE: WHO AM I/EYE?

Chloé asks me, "Why do you study girls, women and feminism? There's never been a problem with your life."
I breathe. Huh.
I smile at her.
"No problems?" I look directly at her.
And I chuckle. There are stories that we talk about and others I do not want to talk about, yet.
What do I tell Chloé? When is a good time to tell her about "problems?" I know her problems will not necessarily be mine. What can she learn from hearing problem stories? Who gains? When as her mother do I share silenced stories? We have begun our conversation. So what is the problem?
As a teacher I look and listen for a teachable moment. We talk about what we watch in relation to possible meaning as we author our lives. As a researcher I am intentional in sustaining a space to linger, to slow down time to think about what is seen and heard. I know I watch and listen with intensity. I know my work did not just come from nowhere. I have written through/with/against my sexed identity, reflecting on experiences of my body since my girlhood. I watch, and I have learned to attend to gender, identity, and to employ a frame of suspicion while engaging in "unruly practices" (Fraser, 1989). What matters in my life and the lives of these girls means speaking about the often unspeakable: the politics of the body; the pleasure and pain experienced as bodied persons.
As a graduate student of curriculum, I think about knowledge claims made about/on/through/against/with girls. Who makes knowledge claims: journalists, psychologists, sociologists, educators? I wonder what sense Chloé makes as she looks at my book shelves. I see an extensive influence of women's words and women's photographs. I listen to her question of why and find myself questioning again: What is the problem? Why study girls? I wonder if Chloé subscribes to a postfeminist position that tells us "the women are all right." I think that we are just beginning to figure out the lives of girls. And as a researcher I am mindful about how I am doing research and I ask myself: why I am doing research; why girls?; and who I am in constructing a re/presentation with girls?
I am mindful to educative and "miseducative experiences" (Dewey, 1904, 1938). I watch inside and outside of schools. I hear school stories from Chloé, her friends, and parents at her school. I work as a researcher in schools. Education conversations are much on my mind. As a mother I watch from the outside. I try to look in, be invited to see. But it is hard. What I hear are stories of abusive practices by those in power. The reproduction of abusive

practice presses discomfort on my body and is calibrated by experience, almost like a measuring instrument for difference, so discomfort is informative and offers a starting point for new understanding (Bateson, 1994, p. 15). I am troubled with what I see as miseducative experiences. These experiences frame my knowing and make me question what is seen. I question my discursive practices of seeing and how that influences my narrative knowing. I would be pretentious to think that I can "see through," "see clearly," or "ascertain." However, I can describe and show.

I always wanted to be a photographer. I mean a "real" photographer, not just in my research work, but in the larger public. My opportunity came when Ronna telephoned asking if I would like to be the "official photographer" for a Hope Foundation fundraiser. This was a first-time photographing, in a larger public. This was a luncheon for about 250 people at the fundraiser. I feel comfortable behind the camera, a source of companionship, holding a hand to enter an unfamiliar place. Holding my camera means my gaze captures the people knowingly or not. I asked people about being photographed; other times I watched and snapped. I captured posed shots: ones of Tommy Banks in conversation and of his fingers dancing on the piano keys; ones of presentations for people being publicly acknowledged; and ones of people talking and visiting.

In high school I read *Life* magazine. I liked the full-page glossy pictures and wondered if I might recreate some of those photo-journalistic images. I imagined myself as a photo-journalist photographing private experiences, the missed, distorted stories from the dark brought to light. I created black and white photographs in the dark room, hours of pleasure in making visible the invisible. This research is a frame of coming to know self as a teacher educator while questioning my practice of seeing.

## WHAT MATTERS

What matters makes a problem out of everything:

> a problem
> > a puzzle
> > a dilemma
> > a riddle
> > a question
>
> > > to be fixed?
> > > answered?

Demanding that girls be considered not only changes what is studied and what becomes relevant to investigate, but it challenges the existing disciplines politically. Girls have not been omitted through forgetfulness or mere prejudice. The structural sexism of most academic disciplines contributes actively to the production and perpetuation of gender hierarchy. What I learn about the world and people is ideologically patterned within a prescribed conformity of a social order that is produced and reproduced. Studying girls is not just about girls, but about the culture and ideological schemata that sustains a regime of power in the world, namely those of class and those of race. I am not attempting to replace/substitute gender with class or race, but I want to challenge authoritative cultural scripts in the making of girl culture.

I wonder about questions of research issues, membership of movements/canons/fields and the question of what is a girl? What is an educated girl? What matters to them? These questions are posed not to straitjacket the studies of girls, but to open and go in search.

As an educational researcher, I talk with girls about what matters to them. I do not exclude myself. As a teacher and as a researcher I reflect on what I evade, dismiss, ignore when I see and hear stories girls tell me. I need to be present fully to hear and see what girls tell me, and then responsibly, I might, hopefully, retell and re/present the shared understanding for change among the girls and myself. I promised the girls that they would be engaged in the re/presentation of this research. I was mindful in my protocol of place as researcher, and I shared studies about girls with the girls in this visual research.

Sadker and Sadker (1980, 1994) and Gaskell, McLaren, and Novogrodsky (1989) report that female culture and public school contexts reflect traditional androcentric beliefs that create inequality for girls and women. Recent reports of teaching may be inadequate for problems undermining adolescent girls' education (American Association of University Women Educational Foundation, 1992; Gilligan, Lyons, & Hanmer, 1990; Holmes & Silverman, 1992). Girls enter school as feminized bodies, a sign, suggesting that girls go through a "crisis of self esteem" at the crossroads of puberty (Brown & Gilligan, 1992; Gilligan, 1987, 1991; Orenstein, 1994; Pipher, 1994). Who does not go through a crisis at puberty? But for girls, the authors tell us, it is all different. We go from being tough, loud and strong girls to becoming demure, quiet, and self-conscious adolescents. These theories frame one knowing of girlhood.

I see girls' lives as simpler, more sincere, before we have to think of ourselves as sexual bodies, before our bodies become "womanly," the focus of outside criticisms, outside lusts, outside evaluation (Bach, 1993, 1995;

Bordo, 1991; Brownmiller, 1986; Fine & Macpherson, 1995; Fine & Zane, 1991; Rubin, 1994; Walkerdine, 1989, 1990; Wolf, 1990;). As I reflect, I wonder: does any body actually go through a simple and naive period? It seems that our girlhood stories are immersed with exposure to sex at too early an age: genital exposure by the man next door, the guy jerking off in the car who called us over, the copies of Playboy seen in homes, older boys trying to look up our skirts before we even knew how to touch ourselves "down there." Our girlhoods may not have been made of tragedy and abuse, but were they made of "sugar and spice?" Since riot grrls put the growl back into girlhood, the meaning of girl has changed. I realize how much the girl-trend has saturated my thoughts as I look at popular culture, bookstores, and research.

One way I can come, literally, to my senses is by seeing the images that the girls produced. Then, by listening to their voices, I have come to know however different my life is from theirs. These are my insights, my composition of reuniting the girl with her body and attending to the girl-in-body, the lived bodily experience of the girl. I have had to learn to see myself through multiple eyes:

> Women have had to learn to be attentive to multiple demands, to tolerate frequent interruptions, and to think about more than one thing at a time. This is a pattern of attention that leads to a kind of peripheral vision which, if you limit roles to separate contexts, you may not have. Sometimes this multiplicity can be confusing and painful, but it can also become a source of insight. (Bateson, 1994, p. 97)

The visual narratives in this research help me remember my own fierce inner-girl. I also experienced the loss of this fierceness with a stormy entry to womanhood. Throughout my work, I found, through my senses, that fierceness, the means to watch and see what matters. For me, "the experience of pleasure and pain is what gives life meaning and gives moral questions their terrible weight. It is the reason that everything matters" (Bach, Kennedy, & Mickelson, 1997, p. 16).

## AN EXAMPLE

Behind the school doors in the orange Camero, their lighthearted voices giggled as they shared a joint. She took one last toke. "It's history." Throwing the roach out of the car window into the school parking lot, he pulled out the Zig Zag papers with a nickel bag of pot. "I'll roll another joint here, and then let's go down to the park." "To hell with school, it sucks anyway." With an hour for lunch plus a spare class immediately following, leaving school seemed too easy. Besides she knew her boyfriend would always drive her back in time for her outdoor physical education class, if she really wanted to be in class. Spring was sneaking in, and the sun seemed even hotter behind the car window; she took another blast, kissed her boyfriend, grinning, "Ya, I'm outta here."

Off they drove. The grey school building was left for the outdoors, for sitting on the side of a hill overlooking the river. The park, located several blocks from the high school, was just far enough to get away from the institutional ethos, an excuse to be outside. The park was a place of solidarity, a private space, a transient space when school classrooms seemed too awful to contemplate. In these habits they resembled their peers, having lost everything in the way of certainty, faithful to skipping uninteresting classrooms for the park and river with the obsessiveness of many of their friends. They were not alone; sex, drugs, rock and roll thrived in their high school years of the late 70s.

The sound of an old muffler rolling into the parking lot startled her back to the thoughts of the reality of school. "Oh shit!" The rusty blue van pulled up, which meant that lunch and the first afternoon classes were over. Oh well, her friends from the gang had arrived ready to party. It was just another Friday night. "Who wants a beer?" shouted a manly looking boy hurrying out of the van. "Fuck the class." She snuggled her boyfriend, he held her closer, hugged her one more time. "Ya, it's Friday, no one will notice." "Ya, right." He rolled another joint and invited the gang to come down to the picnic table by river's edge. The music of "Foghat" blared from the van's stereo speakers, the guitar pumping the pulse of what might lie ahead. Some sensual promise seemed to hang in the air, but what and where, what action would take place, eluded them for now.

She was a "good" girl who loved the socialization of school life. She wanted to know about the things that interested her. She excelled in the arts. She avoided academics. She wondered who liked conjugating verbs anyway. She wanted knowledge, knowledge that connected to her life, the life she was living. She was also a model who had her own money. Beloved and well-cared for by her family and her boyfriend of a year, she, too, loved them all. After dinner on Friday night she performed her daily feminine chores. She curled her straight hair into a

Farrah Fawcett look alike, applied a smidgen of make-up, polished her nails and popped her yellow birth control pill, which she had been taking for nearly a year. She studied herself in the mirror, smiling as she slipped on her boyfriend's old faded jean jacket. Lovely. She was ready for "IT," a fulfilling evening of partying and committed sex; after all, they were a couple.

Tonight the sports car pulled up on time, being late annoyed her, although it never bothered him. Her parents busied themselves with the supper dishes, reminding her once again to be home by 12:30, a curfew that, curiously enough, she always respected. Again she was instructed not to drive with boys who had been drinking. Her father would pick her up if needed. Repeatedly she was instructed, "Please be careful." Hugging her parents goodbye, her father's stern words of "don't get pregnant" had become inessential. She knew his words of warning, he wasn't just making conversation, but she answered, "Yes." To tell the truth she knew she had done wrong in the eyes of her Christian father; he had always treated sex with suspicion, certainly premarital sex was inherently sinful. She wondered what he would say or think if he knew she found sex pleasurable, enjoyable, even fun. She knew she was lucky, possibly smart, not to have gotten pregnant. She nodded, checked the clock and ran out the door. And that was the end of that.

## RE-TELLING A LIVED STORY

My "an example" story has been told and retold; it is a telling telling story. At the time I was 17, now I am 37. So much has happened. As a teacher and a researcher I think about my life as a fierce girl, and the words that Woolf (1929) said to an audience 69 years ago addresses stories around my life as a girl and the evaded curriculum: "When a subject is highly controversial and any question about sex is that, one can only show how one came to hold whatever opinion one does hold" (p. 5). Her words allow my story of being a girl to be told in multiple ways. For me, it is not a narrative of personal disaster and redemption: it is an exploration of how, what and why we need to study girlhood stories that unveil the evaded curriculum: stories with substance use, sexual activity, and contraceptive use. Throughout my work I use the term "evaded curriculum," which was introduced in the American Association of University Women Educational Foundation (AAUW) (1992) report *How schools shortchange girls*:

[Evaded curriculum is] matters [that are] central to the lives of students and teachers but touched upon briefly, if at all, in most schools. These matters include the functioning of bodies, the expression and valuing of feelings, and the dynamics of power. In both formal course work and in the informal exchanges among teachers and students, serious consideration of these areas is avoided. (p. 75)

Style (1993) illuminated the evaded curriculum for me in her key note address from her work-in-progress at a AAUW conference at Mills College. In teaching stories she surfaced one part of the evaded curriculum, that of recognizing and remembering the "web of connection." Her personal teaching stories uncovered the interconnections of gender politics based on race, sex, sexual orientation and religion as it affected her and her individual students' lives.

I tell and retell girlhood stories embedded in gender politics of Western adolescent love and romance, one that re/presents the practice of Western femininity, of the "beauty myth" (Wolf, 1990), a "tradition of imposed limitations" (Brownmiller, 1986, p. 14), a "reproducer of the docile body of femininity" (Bordo, 1991, p. 25). I write my school stories with the missing authority of the feminine, stories of evaded issues where silence is dismissed (Clandinin, Davies, Hogan, & Kennard, 1993; Connelly & Clandinin, 1990). Writing untold stories and not knowing what to speak during the crossroads of my stormy entry into womanhood helped me find the girl within, to re/remember who I was. Writing my stories of school called me to consider the evaded curriculum in my education, a curriculum that would not embrace the daily life experiences I lived as an adolescent girl, a curriculum escaped by not talking, listening or understanding: remembering that with determination or intentionality to not talk about something is to talk about it.

In my research, I attempt to untangle questions about the evaded curriculum within the lives of girls, curriculum that abstains from lived experiences, one that distorts and avoids a commitment to life by disconnecting dimensions of our told stories, a curriculum that silences life: "To be silent about the realities of our interdependent lives when we teach and structure curriculum is to institutionally dismiss them as lesser, inconsequential, not worth noticing" (Style, 1993).

I retell my story as one of being a "bad girl" (Tucker, 1994) who lived tensions inside and outside of school. My home curriculum included lessons on intimacy, marriage and love interwoven with the Judeo-Christian suppression of sexuality and fear of the body as a source of pleasure and beauty. My school curriculum evaded issues central to the health and well-being of my adolescent lived experiences. I have come to see how my life script had been relegated to a heterosexual feminine role, a tightly held category that created tensions between rules of entitlement over my body and the authority on the feminine (Wittig, 1992).

As a researcher and a teacher, I remember how I acted and reacted to dimensions of the evaded curriculum in the classroom and the research process (Bach, 1993, 1995, 1997a; Bach, Clandinin & Greggs, 1992), of how I stopped the talk that addressed the life experiences of sexuality, race, ablism, substance use, and suicide. I remember my student sex education curriculum creating a double-bind. On the one hand, the popular media encouraged me to explore and embrace uncharted sexual totality; on the other hand, adults in authority treated that unknown territory as if it were already mapped and found dangerously unfit for human habitation so that curiosity was seen at best foolish and at worst immoral. Women and girls in this culture live with sexual fear like an extra skin. Each of us wears it differently, depending on our race, class, sexual preference and community; but from birth, we have been taught our lessons well. Reclaiming my stories, breaking the silences by speaking and writing, has allowed me to understand with greater clarity who I am in relation to others in my life.

In retelling my story, I wonder what a curriculum out of the "textbook of my life," the term used by MacIntosh (1992), would have looked like? What discourse of sexuality might render possibilities for our children's lives? Who determines what sexual behaviors will be tolerated? If adolescents meet the norms of their peers, not the norms of others in positions of authority, will they feel the same entitlement as I did in making choices about their bodies, about sex, and about intimate relationships? Who defines the meanings of entitlement to/over/with girls' lives? As a researcher and as an educator, I explore stories of the evaded curriculum in the lives of girls. What boundaries of entitlement are teenage girls experiencing? How do girls understand autonomy, intimacy, and relationships? What do girls have to say about what they see?

## EVADE/EXPERIENCE

evade

one antonym of experience is evade

what's held in the body?
what's showing at the convergence of
bodily experience

and re/presentation?
skirting
the body
sidestepping what is showing?
i
avoid and dodge
seeing


i
search to find ways of
acknowledging
an artificial division
between public and private
the metaphor
the sign
one of fiction, a construct

piece by piece i see experience
in my body
invigorated by evasions
encounters
hurried with feeling
bodily knowledge
pressing me to see
what's ignored
rejected
as a site of
contest

interrupting the
rawness
of
ignorance
the
greenness
of
immaturity
the
loss
of what is
missed

what shapes my vision?
those external representations
those fictions
those stories
those constructs
that evade experience

## From Eyes Wide Shut to a Visual Researcher

As a researcher and student of curriculum, I think about my limited position in the institution. I question what frames my knowing and who I am in
this search. I am mindful to having my eyes turned in and that studying
myself has meant learning to turn my eyes in by turning the lens on myself.
Looking back is difficult. These reflections layer and layer my frames of
knowing as I listen and understand what the girls show me in their camerawork. Turning the lens on self is a way to seriously play, imagine and trouble
self-reflexivity. When I see photographs, I see what matters and learn to see
anew. I learn to tell my stories in different ways.

In a workshop on phototherapy with Judith Weiser, I worked with students of art therapy, practicing psychologists and social workers to better
understand the place of photography while working with people. I wanted
to use what I learned in my narrative inquiry. I wanted the girls to be the
imagemakers of their stories and I hoped to provide a space for them to
make a textbook of their lives, a possibility to document, reflect and imagine. In the workshop, I learned about various practices of photography.
Over the 3 days, we worked through Weiser's (1993) textbook *Phototherapy
techniques: Exploring the secrets of personal snapshots and family albums* and
explored suggested exercises. I was away from home, in another place, away
from family and the necessary interruptions of daily life. In one field text
I wrote,

> Day one...I'm working hard at remaining objective, reasonable, as I
> figure out who I am as the researcher, along with all the other things
> in my life. I'm not working in the same place as these people and I
> think about how I got here....I'm not into letting my inside out and I
> am trying hard to remain distant, cool and even removed. Beginnings
> are hard. I hate beginning with the personal right away, especially with
> people I don't know. In doing the predetermined exercises I watch and
> see others telling sad, hurtful personal stories. I heard stories I had not
> expected. What are we trying to figure out? I feel sick from hearing

stories of abuse. I see the rapid opening of emotions of people who have been hurt. I'm surprised by the openness and the quick pace of opening up. No way am I opening up….Judy speaks of the trust and relationship in getting to deep pockets of meaning. And I think of time. I hears stories of people who claim transformation. I doubt but then again I want to believe what they say…I struggle to remain unemotional, not wanting to feel, and I am suspect. Judy knows from her experiences of over 20 years of working with photography and counselling that I am resisting. I feel like I am floating, that I am not grounded, who am I right now? Who was I yesterday? Who will I be tomorrow? I don't really want to look at myself here in public. I watch and listen closely. I wondered why some told stories publicly and what would family members say if they heard. I feel discomfort on my body….Day three….Judy asked me about my decision of choosing one photograph over another in a death exercise. I cracked. I was annoyed with myself. I couldn't push back the tears as they pushed their way up from my throat. As I looked I could not answer certainly not publicly.

Being part of this workshop, I learned how cameraworks evoke different emotions and stories of possibility and of impossibility. I began to see how photography was embodied in my story and how it re/presented a sensory form of knowing. I was situated within a story and photography that pressed me to question my practices of looking.

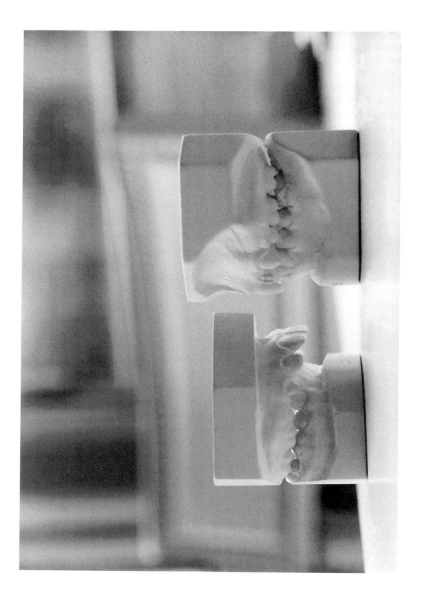

Projective photograph

Making metaphors
Working with self portraits

Photograph of self taken by others
Collecting culture

Family photograph

## MY BODY THROUGH A PHD

Our bodies are sensory-motor systems that generate the excess force which makes them able to move themselves, systems that move toward objectives they perceive, that code their own movements. Our bodies are also substances that can be moved and that can be coded. Subjected to regulated operations of force, our bodies become subjects of capacities, skills, and inclinations; they can be made use of. In and through operations of force, the bodies of speakers become identified, coded, and significant. Discourse is elaborated about them. Language is itself power; the determination of what is said, in what codes, to whom, and in what circumstances organizes a power structure about interlocutors. (Lingis, 1994, p. 53)

my body

a some body

a body
writing
photographing
workingworkingworkingworkingworkingworkingworkingworkingwork-
ingworkingworkingworkingworkingworkingworkingworkingworkingwork-
ingworkingworkingworkingworkingworkingworkingworkingworkingwork-
ingworkingworkingworkingworkingworkingthrough a ph.d
with blurred identities, flowing through
student
teaching assistant / research assistant
scholarship winner
volunteer
mother/lover/daughter/sister/friend

as i trouble my script, mess up the house
change the cover
search for the missing
losing part of my self
a body that invites

a
lump
a lump of tears

breastbreastbreastbreastbreastbreastbreastbreastbreastbreastbreastbreast-
breastbreastbreastbreastbreastbreastbreastbreast......mammogram/ultr
asound/ultrasound/mammogram/breast exam
lumps of tears
     and fear
animosity
no anesthetic no drugs
     a small cut
     flesh
     my breast
        blood trickled
dripping gently
pulsating through a biopsy
     stitch,stitch, stitch, stitch, stitch, stitch
        taped/bandage
           some sense of discomfort
           bewilderment
           what just happened
           need sleep
           but i can't sleep
           worryworryworryworry
           in silence
           hidden by laughter
           leaves me sleepless
           fearing
           desiring calm

    waitingwaitingwaitingwaitingwaitingwaitingwaitingwaitingwaitingwait-
ingwaitingwaitingwaitingwaitingwaitingwaitingwaitingwaiting to hear
benign/good/harmless

the favorable word raises a lump of tears
some sleep
some calm
just one more mammogram/ultrasound
just one more to be safesafesafesafesafesafesafesafesafe

a moment of repose
a body at
peace for a while

begins with a sneeze/cold/flu/fever
feverfeverfever
chillsweat          bronchitisssssss
                                  fatigueeeeeeee
pain
pain
thumb pain
fingers hurt
hand pain
wrist pain
pain
pain physiotherapy
          physiophysio
          physiophysiophysiophysiophysiophysiophysiophy

                                   quiet
                                   anger
                                   tearstearstearstears

                         pain
                         again
                    bad back pain
                     lower pain
                     a stiffness
                 a death in the body

                         drugs
                       medicated
                         drugs
                          pain
                     sleeplessness
                       sleeplessness
                     sleeplessness

    xray
          fracture
          tears
                    anger
                              drugsdrugsdrugs
                                          sleeplessness

some pain
some
peace
at last some strength

i feel nothing without the physical body

## CAN THERE BE A CURRICULUM OF EXPERIENCE?

I start the dishwater, turn on the dryer, feed the cats, let the dog out and wave goodbye to my family who will be back in about 3 hours, a moment. In this moment, I ask myself, and imagine, what a curriculum of experience might look like? What experience is worthwhile? Whose experience is seen? Who interrupts the rawness of ignorance, the greenness of immaturity, the loss of what is missed? What is a worthwhile curriculum for girls? What does it mean to be an educated girl? an educated woman? Who decides how bodies ought to live their lives? What acquired subject knowledge might influence a curriculum of experience?

Now we have the problem of discovering the connection which actually exists within experience between the achievements of the past and the issues of the present. We have the problem of ascertaining how acquaintance with the past may be translated into a potent instrumentality for dealing effectively with the future. We may reject knowledge of the past as the end of education and thereby only emphasize its importance as a means. When we do that we have a problem that is new in the story of education: How shall the young become acquainted with the past in such a way that the acquaintance is a potent agent in appreciation of the living present? (Dewey, 1938, p. 23)

What past experiences shape my present vision? How have the achievements of my past and the issues of the present influenced what I look at? These questions of past and future press me to think about my present practices in authoring my life as a beginning teacher educator. I know my interpretations are framed by my past experiences, present understanding and projective possibilities for my future, all of which frame an important understanding of who I am in relation to other's lives. I think and watch what is acknowledged in relation to curriculum. What matters to whom? I have learned whose vision has been excluded, dismissed, distorted and misrepresented.

In a *Room of one's own*, Woolf (1929) argues that "a woman must have a room of her own if she is to write fiction." I connect this to my own lived stories as a woman who wants to write those stories of lived experiences that touch upon economic oppression, male scholarship, feminist scholarship, traditions in women's writings, authority in women's relationships with women, and women's discourse. Presently, I have some money, a room, and time. As a graduate student my understanding of curriculum lingers in my mind. I cannot imagine a single overarching curriculum that is responsible for all girls. I see curriculum contingent on the negotiated intentions, and while different curricula may support the same intentions of education, precisely how those intentions are lived out is a matter of further negotiation. In my view, where negotiation is evaded, dominant cultural scripts set a singular curricular agenda of what happens to girls. What epistemological constraints are determined in the structuring of a curriculum? How does a curriculum look when we use already interpreted language that brings with it the already constructed metaphors, signs and story. How might we interrupt and mess up the scripts of girlhood? How can girls' evaded experiences inform curriculum in readdressing conditions that have shaped our knowledge claims? Girl is the visual sign but not a straightforward signifier:

> The politics of girl culture is a politics of metaphor: it deals in the currency of signs and is, thus, always ambiguous. For the subcultural milieu has been constructed underneath the authorized discourses, in the face of the multiple disciplines of the family, the school and the workplace. Subcultures forms up in the space between surveillance and the evasion of surveillance, it translates the fact of being under scrutiny into the pleasure of being watched. It is hiding in the light. (Hebdige, 1988, p. 35)

I think about the way that gender has been encoded and how that affects girls' lives. I wonder about the taken-for-granted experiences of hiding in the light. In my view, curriculum ought to be seen over/through/against a life being lived. I see curriculum at once being constructed and reconstructed through storied narratives of experience, concealed by gaps, those necessary spaces for the unknown, uncertainty and surprise that comes with watching, looking and seeing. Curriculum is a "life's course of action" (Pinar, 1976), pictured through lived experience, "a process of living out the stories we tell ourselves in order to make meaning of our experience" (Connelly & Clandinin, 1988).

I press my understanding of curriculum to look at stories that actively shape my experience in relation to what is evaded in lived experiences. I am intentional in reading the untold, unseen and unheard experience of the absence from or distortions in curricular texts. Curriculum means inviting in the diversity of students' lives and teachers' lives and cultures. I think back and reread texts from the "cries and whispers" of female life histories, and in reading fragments of foremothers, I trouble my understanding of curriculum through/against women's and girls' histories. Whose theory? Whose story? Questions of the nature of knowledge and whose knowledge is legitimated are much on my mind.

Questions of what it means to be an educated woman have long been with us (Rich, 1979; Roland Martin, 1982, 1986). I think about what it means to be an educated girl? What is an adequate ideal of the educated girl? For Roland Martin (1982), "The educated person must join thought to action, and reason to feeling and emotion....To do this the educational realm must be reconstituted to include the reproductive processes of society" (p. 147). Many women write and question the knowledge that is constructed (Belenky, Clinchy, Goldberger, & Tarule, 1986; Grumet, 1988; Jaggar & Bordo, 1992; Kristeva, 1986; Ruddick, 1989) What counts as knowledge (Code, 1987, 1991, 1992)? What is science (Harding, 1986; Keller, 1985)? I see this present work as part of my past, and this reading assists me in making sense of my life. I ask myself, "How do I live my life with new directions in relation to my past and present?" What am I creating as I write my life within personal and public sites? I remember our foremothers, our foregatherers, who have recorded life histories, a promise for inclusion, a holistic way of being and becoming within a curriculum of experience. I am hopeful that by continuing to write and remember the cries and whispers of women like Aphra Behn (1640–1689), Harriet Martineau (1802–1876), Margaret Fuller (1810–1850), Barbara Bodichon (1827–1891), Lucy Stone (1818–1893), Matilda Joslyn Gage (1826–1898), Josephine Butler (1828–1906), Hedwig Dohn (1833–1919), Millicent Garrett Fawcett (1847–1929), Charlotte Perkins Gilman (1860–1935), Emma Goldman (1869–1940), Olive Schreiner (1855–1920), Vida Goldstein (1869–1949), Christabel Pankhurst (1880–1958), Alice Paul (1885–1977), Vera Brittain (1896–1970), Mary Ritter (1876–1958), and Simone de Beauvior (1908–) that I will never forget.

It is difficult work. Making change is not easy. Reforming equal access to education for women and girls is challenging and important work, today, just as it was for Wollstonecraft (1792): "It is useless, to seek reform for women alone, without speaking about a general reformation of all society" (p. 31). I think about curriculum as reflecting diverse lives lived inside and outside of the classroom, knowing that our education system supports the practice of specialization and requires a process of selection. This means that from a comparatively early age crucial areas of knowledge become alien, other peoples' business. This exclusive learning process, together with competitive practice, ensures that we begin our progress towards social and economic independence by developing defensive positions which discourage dialogue and intervention from outside. Any attempt to redefine the educated person in the manner the future requires, without also addressing the long-standing value hierarchy that places the public sphere above the private, productive processes above reproductive, and men above women, is futile. We cannot expect people to endorse an education in traits and qualities they consider suspect....Educators cannot by themselves transform our culture's attitudes and expectations....We can become aware of and try to counteract the negative messages transmitted by the standard curriculum about women and their culturally associated tasks and traits. (Roland Martin, 1986, p. 10)

With this in mind I continue to be interested in challenging entrenched beliefs about femininity. What origins of women's and girls' thinking connect with my present understandings of curriculum? I believe, through a curriculum of experience, girls might become independent, free in mind and body. I want girls' lives to matter:

The facts of the body both separate and connect. They testify to the links between human beings and other mammals and living systems, but they divide the sexes and the developmental stages. The body's truths are often concealed, so it is not always easy to learn about birth or sex or death, or the curious and paradoxical relationships between them. We keep them separate and learn about them on different tracks, just as we learn separately about economics and medicine and art, and only peripheral vision brings them together. Experience is structured in advance by stereotypes and idealizations, blurred by caricatures and diagrams. (Bateson, 1994, pp. 4–5)

As I reflect on my life I am aware that neither way of thinking is politically neutral. I hear the words of "reform" and "backlash" and words of those in positions of authority whose pedagogy continues to advocate theories that female education is to render girls as "victim." I see how sex-differentiated theories in education and existing gender differentiation result in an educational system that sustains political and hegemonic norms that perpetuate the exclusion and misrepresentation of women and girls (Aisenberg &

Harrington, 1988; Gaskell & McLaren, 1987; Gaskell, McLaren, & Novogrodsky, 1989; hooks, 1984). I believe stories of exclusion and misrepresentation keep girls from exercising their minds/bodies. And I wonder what curricular pathways can be authored as we write our lives and make meaning of our lived experiences. Will feelings of alienation and fragmentation continue to be lived out by other women and those girls who experience classrooms of "chilly climates?" Did you feel invited in your classes or silenced? Did your teachers not only hear your voice, but see how you said things? Were there conversations about class, race, ability? What imaginings might be possible in spaces that embrace difference? How will I impact those I teach as I disrupt the representational story as I tell my research story?

I will be hopeful that the sounds of silence are interpreted through multiple ways of knowing. I will wonder what we are re/producing in schools and campuses within our global context. What images of women and girls will be mirrored in a formal curriculum? Is "connected knowing" valued—if so how? What will be the arrangement of the work within the "classroom as curriculum?" I wonder if girls will feel uncomfortable in large classrooms, working in groups, perhaps still sitting in rows? I wonder what issues of control and power will have been "evaded" at school? A curriculum of experience needs to reinforce self-knowledge and emotional experience.

Perhaps, then, I will acknowledge the possibility of a curriculum of experience that flickers.

# Notebook 2

For me, photography is a site of vulnerability for the photographer, for those photographed and for those who look at photographs. In coming to terms with my sense making in the photo-gathering, photo-taking, and photo-viewing, I engaged in "writing the light" as a way to frame my questions about the use of photography, about our sense of sight, and about how peripheral visions inform my thinking.

This shifting and switching define in part how the visual is approached in visual narrative. The literal interpretation of "visual" implies the eyes and the sense of sight. Western tradition has depended largely on sight to determine the meaning of things; however, a definition based solely on sight cannot account for nuances and details noticed by the other senses. For example, we can never say we know what a rutabaga is just by looking because one swift smell can conjure up the horror of the memories associated with eating this particular food. In this sense, I used images to create uncomfortable narratives and dialogues within the real of girls' texts to maintain a level of ambiguity within my understanding. Thinking of the girls' words in terms of the visual points is a way to emphasize details resulting from an awareness of the shifting nature of meaning around something real. The visual is used to resist others' desires for clear identities. This notebook is an exploration of subjectivity, a place to view the reflections of the girl's bodies as the primary images for use in reconsideration of their symbolic worlds.

This explanation of the relationship between language and body also describes the interaction between desire and biology. It is a discussion about the association of disparate parts into one body or the process of making girl culture. Lingering images of bewilderment and feeling discomfort inform my knowing and my standpoint of observation, momentarily. A situated position in which to stand so that my world can envelop, split, and multiply. My point of view can be understood as both the experienced "I" and the "eye" that "looks out" and optically defines the public space and ramifications unique to photography in this visual narrative research:

When we look through our physical eye we are forced to accept that the perceived reality is always, by necessity, framed by the mechanics of vision. More recent theories have explained this optical illusion and inform us that retinal image can never be compared to the actual object, we are unable to "see" outside the world of imitations, of representations. If we imagine this mechanism duplicated by the camera lens then a photographer is caught within a double bind. There is both the recognition of the limitations of the optical frame and a drive to capture the "object of desire". Through this scopic vision our outwardly shared experience is not lived, but imaged; internalised as a more enduring replacement for the "real". (Brettle & Rice, 1994, p. 4)

I have troubled the use of the first person through multiple personas and voices, inhabiting different thought and moments. The stages of identity formation are sensual, commonplace, and often close to home: standing in the mirror; stiffening at the hands of a knife; discerning the pleasant scent or fear of a hand caressing the shoulders. I have blended fictional and theoretical approaches that address subjectivity across categories of sex, class, gender, and ethnicity. The use of the first person is not self-congratulatory nor a lament for a lost or post-self nor a site of an essential self. Nor will readers find "self" depicted as a storehouse of accumulated knowledge. As a composer I celebrate the pleasures as well as the struggles and invite multiple readings. At times I drift through memory, speaking to the complex task of mining the site of subjectivity.

I could not envisage how each girl would respond to photographing. The engagement the girls had with the cameraworks left room for unpredictable, even eccentric discoveries, for openings not closures. What appears first are photographs that embody autobiography and stories of the evaded. The visual narrative text is produced at the crossroads between the act of photographing and composing a story as an attempt to bring together educational critique and girls' experiences. This notebook attends to making the private public and the possibility of seeing the evaded in the girls' daily lives. I have intentionally created a state of vulnerability for them and the stories they tell of their photographs by extending the dialogue about how they perceive themselves. By making the evaded public I came to know "intimacy is sacred-packed with boundaries, limits, assumptions, privatization, silences, isolation and an area in which seemingly innocent decisions are made in danger" (Brettle & Rice, 1994, p. 4).

## SEEING THE HYPHEN

I bolt home, peddle as fast as I can
I like the rush of going fast, swerving up, and jumping curbs
I think about what I just heard

                        I see
                        hear it again as
I relisten to a flood of voices, seeing again their faces,
remembering how they move their bodies
I wonder has my gentle oppression
defined the problem
missed the subtle insinuation
          working inside my head, did I say enough?
               was I deep enough?
               tough enough?
You tell me,
those who love it, those who doubt
You cannot know how I got here
You cannot see how I feel

       Still who might hear and feel the story
                        differently

do I count tears, hurt, silence

               how am I supposed to feel

               after I hear their words

               what I dare not tell

Will they hear what I have to say
as the truth, the real, the authentic
what experience makes sense
what matters
learning to understand the turning inside out, outside in

what is in that tear drop of fire
of wetness moisture
a tranquillity of knowing a wrong, a loss
that lump that moves up my throat
I pinch myself, quick I won't raise the tears, I don't want to see
and I wonder where does the story of the tear go?

At times watching scares me
this writing life means seeing
                                        making sense of thinking unthinkable
finding an escape knowing there is
No way to hide
                              in the light
knowing I have scratched the surface
                                        perhaps, something  different
can be seen


## VISUAL KNOWING

Life taught me that being an artist was dangerous. (hooks, 1995, p. 1)

Life taught me that being an artist meant living on the margins.
In high school I worked with clay, metals, and fabrics. My visual art's
teacher, Mrs. McCallum, was a white middle-class woman who promoted
and exhibited my art works. I remember her words of praise. This was my
only high school teacher who valued my art interest. Being a student in her
class transferred to valuing what my mother did for a living. My mother is a
painter who continues to paint and show her works in galleries. This art
teacher encouraged me to attend a post-secondary art college. I really
believed her. I spent extra time in the art room. I escaped to her room. After
school and lunch times were productive and pleasurable. I learn by seeing,
talking and doing. This learning space with this art teacher made me believe
that I was an artist. I remember with sadness the day she told me she was
leaving the school.
Growing up in an artist's family frames my visual knowing. Art experiences mattered at home and were cultivated through extra curricular activities; I grew up in art-filled rooms and with trips to galleries. As I read *Art on
my mind: Visual politics*, hooks (1995) offers another telling of the place of
being seen as an artist with her high school story. Not believing that a white
male art teacher understood black people's lives, bell hooks could never

believe that black women could be artists. Her parents influenced her to not see herself as an artist. Her story of difference connects for me as a woman from the standpoint of viewing artistic knowing and career possibilities. My sense making means that "art is on my mind." What happens to girls who find pleasure in the arts? What spaces exist in schools? What knowledge is legitimated?

## FINDING PHOTOGRAPHY'S PLACE

Photographs are substantial shadows. Simultaneously material and immaterial, they are at once signs and objects, documents of actual events, images of absent things, and real things in themselves. They embody a paradox: they are substantive echoes of the first order. For all photographs are, on the one hand, quotations from an irrecoverable text, the world of yesterday, of the hour before last, of the second before this one and on the other hand they are ghostly emanations from the real what Barthes once called the spectrum of the photograph-light radiating from an object captured on light sensitive emulsion through a combination of chemical and mechanical means. (Hebdige, 1988, p. 13)

This visual research offers a view by girls. The photographs reproduced in this book should not be regarded as an afterthought or supplement designed passively to illustrate stories put forward in the research text. The photographs taken by the girls form and serve to pose, from the margins, one of my central wonders about the images that bind this book together. The ontological status of the photograph is always equivocal (Barthes & Bazin, cited in Mitchell, 1992). But who is making the constructions, re/presentations, documenting and making knowledge claims?

As a researcher working with girls, I question who gets to take the picture? Who is making girl culture? Whose gaze de/constructs a photograph? Who listens to the story told about girls' photographs. Who is doing the talking? My hope is not how to make re/presentation, but how to avoid re/presentation. This matters to me:

What is important now is to recover our senses. We must learn to see more, to hear more, to feel more. Our task is not to find the maximum amount of content in a work of art, much less to squeeze more content out of the work than is already there. Our task is to cut back content so that we can see the thing at all. (Sontag, 1966, p. 34)

The photographs included in these notebooks, irrespective of the quality of the reproductions, include images that haunt me. I question my intentionality when I present and represent the cameraworks. Am I, too, reproducing those practices that criticize? It is as though I have three parallel spools running simultaneously: one with photographs, one with transcript text, and one with associations surfacing from my memory and reading. Viewing the photographs evokes words, although the story is not bound to them. Sometimes the story between images and argument may seem tenuous, but I hope that there is connected knowing, a tension, that necessary tension of theory practice. Connections are always dynamic, dialogic in nature.

Sociological and anthropological researchers have constructed visual documentaries, essays, histories with photography and film (Becker, 1974, 1981; Berger & Mohr, 1982; Collier & Collier, 1986; Harper, 1987, 1989; Herron & Williams, 1996). In approaches to counselling, photography and other forms of visual re/presentation have reframed life experiences within cocounselling contexts (Martin & Spence, 1989; Weiser, 1993). My narrative research (Bach, 1993) draws upon the use of still photography to evoke memory in our lives, a memory around which we construct and reconstruct life stories:

Photography, because it preserves the appearance of an event or a person, has always been closely associated with the idea of the historical. The ideal of photography, aesthetics apart, is to seize an "historic" moment...photographs convey a unique sense of duration. The I am is given its time in which to reflect on the past and to anticipate its future: the exposure time does no violence to the time of the I am: on the contrary, one has the strange impression that the exposure time is the lifetime. (Berger, 1972, p. 47)

Seeing the girls' enjoyment from documenting their daily life with box cameras and talking about their photography, I was struck by the power of reshooting images, of shooting photographs of photographs, and with the girls' revisualizing and retelling their stories. The "acts of photographing" guided our conversations, each viewing allowed for a possibility to see we were different people, learning from difference and from other ways about how to live a life. We talked about the why—why they chose a particular frame to shoot, and why one particular moment of time was responded to rather than another. There was always a story behind the story. The need to see through the story was helpful in understanding the girls' photographs as they became sites to other stories that drifted into and through their daily lives. I found these sites difficult to explain with words or concepts, and this troubles my writing of my visual narrative research. Knowing this, I have borrowed from Spence (1986, 1995) and Weiser (1975) by seeing "photography as a verb." My visual narrative research is a learning experience about girls' daily lives, expressed not just in the passive verb sense of evaluating product-print, but in the active verb sense of learning. I see the making of schoolgirl culture as a way to come to know girls in a different way. Photography slows time into moments, moments that can be studied. As Sontag (1977) writes, "A photograph is not only an image (as a painting is an image), an interpretation of the real; it is also a trace, something directly stenciled off the real, like a footprint or a death mask" (p. 26).

The most pleasurable experience of the girls from my Master's research (Bach, 1993) was having a camera. They enjoyed the act of photographing. What matters, for me, was the girls' excitement at being imagemakers. Their voices and my desire to work visually, with pleasure, pressed me to find photography's place within my narrative inquiry. Speaking autobiographically, photography and research make sense. I see the possibility for understanding photographs with multiple truths. As Spence (1995) writes "An understanding of this frees up the individual from the constant search for the fixity of an 'ideal self' and allows enjoyment of self as process and becoming" (p. 176). The search for self at adolescence is well documented by Gilligan (1987, 1991), Brown and Gilligan (1992), Orenstein (1994), Pipher (1994), and Fine and Macpherson (1995).

Photographs act as a record. By 1839, Henry Fox Talbot perfected the art of chemically fixing a shadow as a way to record images permanently on specifically treated paper "by the agency of light alone, without any aid whatever from the artist's pencil" (Mitchell, 1992, p. 3). My hope is to see in the light and see in the shadows the culture that girls make. The girls tell me that they look and relook at their photographs. Each of the girls has created a textbook of the cameraworks: "The photographs act as a tangible marker of something which could otherwise go back into the unconscious and remain dormant for a long time" (Spence, 1995, p. 176). This happened to me as the researcher. I see the photograph as an artifact that can be read and reread over time. Each reading evokes a different sound, something different is seen and heard. With that difference comes reflections of memories:

Yet, unlike memory, photographs do not themselves preserve meaning. They offer appearances—with all the credibility and gravity we normally lend to appearances—prised away from their meaning. Meaning is the result of understanding functions. And functioning takes place in time, and must be explained in time. Only that which narrates can make us understand. Photographs in themselves do not narrate. Photographs preserve instant appearances. (Berger, 1980, p. 51)

According to Spence (1995), photographs offer us a site to "objectify and see a separate part of ourselves which can be integrated back into the over-all subjectivity, or core self, as when we are ready for it" (p. 176). Although photography objectifies, because visual narrative involves the process of lis-tening to the stories told about photographs, they can also act as "transitional objects" towards another reality. In this sense, they can be seen as stepping stones, perhaps a way of searching for narrative truth.

The camerawork in this visual narrative is amateur, and I understand what Spence (1995) means when she writes about the electrical charge, the energy released in photography: "Symbols are especially powerful for trans-forming the unconscious which does not operate with the language of logic but with images" (p. 166). Each time I looked at the camerawork, it was pos-sible to order and reorder the photographs into a variety of mini-narratives. There is never a fixed story being told, no narrative closure. In constructing a variety of re/presentations, stories moved around, providing an infinity of possible tellings or montages. The photographs start further and more sus-tained conversations. Listening to the girls, I was aware of the cathartic release when they spoke about their cameraworks. I sensed that the girls responded viscerally without the mediation of their intellect.

Visual narrative research makes "visible" different parts or narratives of girls' stories, their subjectivity, as well as enabling us to explore different positions, differing standpoints within a dynamic, and thus one can play with positions of authority. Transformation of fixed or screen memories becomes possible through such forms of constructing the visual narrative. Photographs can help us to acknowledge what has previously been resisted and repressed then let go and move on from the material being worked through; it helps us to unfreeze memories. As well, Spence (1995) believes photographs enable us to come to terms with negativity; photographs can be markers of triumph, a celebration of integration, and the successful explo-ration of an issue or pattern.

I see this in the girls' cameraworks. As well, there is something powerful behind the combination of image and text that forms the composition of my visual narrative research. Spence's (1995) awareness of photography's poten-tial keeps me mindful of whose view is privileged:

What bias does the viewer/reader inflect in the viewing of the picture or in the reading of the text (language is also ideologically biased and can be understood in many ways)? What might be the possible responses of a person who is not part of the social, sexual or racial groups an image is explicitly directed at. All photographs are message carriers, either between members of the same social class who share common codes, or between differing classes and cultures. (p. 39)

In our culture most of the "messages" received by girls are mediated via the dominant culture. What matters, for me, is the reproduction of misrepresented lives. I see most of these messages as privileged, in short, "to salute...and show their identity papers" (Cixous, 1994, p. 51); and in many ways, that means I see theories re/presented as concealing and distorting the relationships of girls with other, and often with each other. What happens if these messages/images are distorted, ignored, and institutionally dismissed?

In photographic image, it is possible to experience a multitude of responses, and yet the impossibility of defining what is "real" remains. It is a matter for debate whether these images will ultimately be replaced by the seamless representations of new technology. Photographic "truth" has never been absolute, but in its various attempts to intervene in and celebrate political and personal lives, it offers access to a particular view of human states. Once we question the photographic "moment of truth," it is possible to consider the moments before and the moments after the shutter is released—we are free to explore the possibility of a photographic "movement" and "intervention" in time (Brettle & Rice, 1994, p. 4). Despite this,

digital imaging dramatically changes the rules of this game. It creates a condition in which the image maker may choose among different devices and procedures for mapping form intensities in a scene to intensities in a display or print, in which image fragments from different sources may quickly and seamlessly be combined, and in which arbitrary inventions in the image-construction process are easy to introduce and difficult to detect. The distinction between the casual process of the camera and the intentional process of the artist can no longer be drawn so confidently and categorically. Potentially, a digital "photograph" stands at any point along the spectrum from algorithmic to intentional...the referent has come unstuck. (Mitchell, 1992, p. 31)

Photography makes obvious the difficulties I have with every variety of "data," of field texts, of this narrative research. I see a continued need for multiple forms of representation of data and research. And finding photography's place is how I have come to understand the place photographs occupy in different ways of telling a story that are controlled by the girls themselves. Visual narratives disrupt and subvert girl culture as a means of reinforcing, documenting, and checking narrative statements. Through their narratives, the girls have given me ways of penetrating the cultural clichés, the view of the archetype characters in myths about girls.

I wonder, is there ever freedom from privilege? I know that what I perceive is only part of the reality before me. Every girl creates her own world, and it is through photography that I learn to see through/with/against other eyes. I have also learned that distortions in understanding girls' cameraworks is inevitable. This means that each girl must be seen in her own story. I can have conversations with the girls and share the realism of their visual world.

## SO HOW DID YOU GET STARTED?

This narrative research is largely a deconstructive project, revealing the elisions, blind spots, loci of the unsayable within visual texts. The girls' visual narratives, pictured through photography and conversations, have been searched and researched, diving deep and surfacing over the 3 years I have questioned the evaded. I looked at curriculum and the places we recognize and remember the web of connections from life stories and photographs. Together we attempt to disrupt and uncover the sign/symbol and give meaning to the evaded curriculum at the "crossroads of adolescent lives" (Brown & Gilligan, 1992, p. 1). I call visual narrative a meditative vehicle because I come to it neither as a map of knowledge nor as a guide to action, nor even for pleasure.

Photographs re/present "selectively framed information" (Weiser, 1993, p. 56). Just as there are many ways for decoding photographs in disciplines of medicine, geology, anthropology, and so forth, the girls told and retold different stories about their photographs as they searched to make meaning, connections and references to the lives they are writing. A person searching for the meaning of a given photograph will never be able to find the truth it holds for anyone else; perhaps in this supposed limitation lies a strength of the camera as a research tool. Each girl had her own camera, film and time to create images. Many of the photographs that they created were stories assigning strong feelings, thinking, and deeply held beliefs told and retold over time. Weiser (1993) and Spence (1995) suggest multiple readings from different viewing at different times. I am aware that each photograph seen in a different context is interpreted very differently.

### Working method

The images, created with photographs, thicken ways of seeing. Images suggest a space for visual re/presentation similar to that of journal entries, field notes, and artifacts better thought of as "field texts" (Clandinin & Connelly, 1994). The visual field texts are constructed by the girls and myself to re/present aspects of life as it unfolds. Through conversations around their photographs we coconstruct a "research text" (Clandinin & Connelly, 1994), one I refer to as a "visual narrative" (Bach, 1996c). These visual narratives show a social life as a process of lived experiences made up of relationships and shared understandings among the girls, their worlds and myself. Ethics were significant in our conversations in relation to photo-taking, photo-viewing and photo-gathering (see "Photographic Ethics: Talking out both sides of your mouth," p. 59).

Each girl used five or more rolls of film, each creating close to 100 images, as a way to document their life stories. The girls' words and their photographs show and tell of lives in relation to the "evaded curriculum" (AAUW, 1992; Style, 1992). Throughout the notebooks I have been borrowing my interpretative understanding of Weiser's (1993) and Spence's (1995) works, as well as their photographic directives, as a way to permit the girls and myself a space and a language to construe our own understanding of the cameraworks in relation to the evaded curriculum. What is evaded for girls when we teach and structure curriculum? What is left silent? What realities from their lives are institutionally dismissed as lesser, inconsequential, or not worth noticing?

## CAMERAWORKS I

### Projective photographs

In the following projective photographs I attempted to deal with the ways I construct meaning from any photograph:

The projective component of understanding photographic meaning underlies all interactions between people and snapshots. Projecting meaning onto the photographs (and anything else our senses encounter) is integral with our looking at them. Photographs simplify by partializing life and help slow time into units of meaning that people can study. In describing and reacting to photos, people are frequently able to reach pockets of strong feelings. (Weiser, 1993, p. 13)

Listening to schoolgirl stories of selected photographs unearthed questions such as: What about a title? What is the story that goes with this photograph? Ask the photograph its name, what it means and whether it has anything to tell you. Is there anyone you know who would like to have this photograph? Consider the thoughts, feelings, memories, and fantasies that you have become aware of in this photograph.

## CAMERAWORKS II

### Making metaphor

### Working with self-portraits

A photograph is not only an image, it holds a story, an interpretation of the real, a trace of life, of something that is held as unchanging. The girls' visual narratives are surrounded by mutually constructed meaning; their photographs point to where they have been as well as to where they might be going. Working with making metaphor evokes a memory in our lives, a memory around which we construct and reconstruct stories.

Berger and Mohr (1982) suggest that

> a photograph is simpler than most memories, its range more limited. Yet, with the invention of photography we acquire a new means of expression more closely associated with memory than any other....Both the photograph and the remembered depend upon and equally oppose the passing of time. Both preserve moments, and propose their own form of simultaneity, in which all their images can coexist. Both stimulate, and are stimulated by, inter-connectedness of events. Both seek instants of revelations, for it is only such instants which give full reason to their own capacity to withstand the flow of time. (p. 280)

Photographs the girls collected focus on daily life, imagination, fantasy, interpersonal relations and fragments of their life stories. I invited the girls to "Go photograph for this moment":

"Your favorite place"
"Your favorite activity"
"Your favorite person"
"Your favorite objects which are special to you"

# CAMERAWORKS III

## Collecting culture

### Self-portraits taken by others

Here the girls were invited to have new photographs created of themselves by a significant other, a space to learn from seeing other perspectives as another way of collecting their culture. I asked them to try to

have someone play at being detective: have them follow you around for a few days photographing you, as if trying to figure out who you are and what you are like from the photographs they take of you. Try not to pose. Then with the second half of the film have the person photograph you as you wish: pose all you want.

If there is a narrative form unique to photography, will it not resemble that of the cinema? Surprisingly, photographs are the opposite of films. Photographs are retrospective and are received as such: films are anticipatory. Before a photograph you search for what was there. In cinema you wait for what is to come next. All film narratives are, in this sense, adventures: they advance, they arrive. The term flashback is an admission of the inexorable impatience of the film to move forward. By contrast, if there is a narrative form intrinsic to still photography, it will search for what happened, as memories or reflections do. Memory itself is not made up of flashbacks, each one forever moving inexorably forward. Memory is a field where different times coexist. The field is continuous in terms of the subjectivity which creates and extends it, but temporarily it is discontinuous. (Berger, 1972, pp. 279–280)

# CAMERAWORKS IV

## Family albums

Here the girls were invited to share existing family album photographs as a "basis for telling stories, and beginning to unmask memories with a...listener" (Spence, 1995, p. 172). The agenda for this cameraworks was established over time and with trust. Within the family album I was shown and heard about those affected by social taboos, divorce, illness and death, those whose daily lives were undervalued, stories of childcare, schooling, housework, and of visiting friends. The experience of those who have tried to take snapshots within institutional contexts foregrounds immediately the problem of the institutional gaze. It offers a useful learning process in relation to forms of external censorship and self-censorship.

Events that could not be photographed at the time can be remembered through the photographs of objects and places that stand in for the persons or objects involved. Family albums bury other people's histories. Seeing them makes possible a space for looking at ideas of universalized experiences and providing a spectrum of markers of identity through the photographs: identities created through family histories of marriage, family rituals, work, class, race, and the evaded aspect of self and family. I was mindful of seeing areas of life that are often photographed, and I troubled the dominant stories of the "good girl" and the "happy family." Taking a look and turning sideways are forms of autobiographical documentation that can be put together and that open the possibility of exploring the contradictory visual markers of sexuality, power relationships and expressions of desire.

## RESEARCH RELATIONSHIPS

i
work hard to
avoid
the invitation of rejection
as a researcher
i
try to
sidestep
possibilities
of
refusal
i try to be a research pleaser

At first I think of my research relationship as one of being true to self, being real, balancing the contradictions of interviewing girls and wanting to be one of them. My intention from the beginning has been that the girls would photograph daily life that would unearth the evaded experiences, and I would listen to the stories they told about them. I provided the girls with cameras, film and developed the girls' photographs for the cameraworks. I had my tape recorder and transcribed tapes and photographs; I was the data collector. As well, during this time, I was a doctoral student in curriculum studies who was armed with educational theories. Being in relation with the girls and using their words and photographs, I began to write a text with/against/through my stories of coming to know girls differently. I am mindful of Code's (1987) assertion that "it is persons who know-not abstracted, isolated intellects, understandings, imaginations, or faculties of reason" (p. 101).

Learning to step out of the student image I have lived with for so long continues to trouble my knowing of self as a researcher. I like research. I like to study people's photographs, and being a researcher means thinking and problematizing the ethical interactions of using photography and its influence on the girls' lives. I watch carefully, as Code (1987) put it:

Thinking individuals have a responsibility to monitor and watch over shifts in, changes in, and efforts to preserve good intellectual practice. Not everyone is either physically able or intellectually equipped to watch over all areas; hence, the necessity for a division of intellectual labor, with the responsibilities this division entails both for experts and for those inclined to take experts at their word. Such a division should not be seen as an excusing feature of epistemic community, everyone is responsible, to the extent of his or her ability, for the quality of cognitive practice in a community. (p. 245)

Who makes the knowledge claims about girls? Who gets to decide? As a researcher, the question of knowing the girls means I am awake to my responsibility to know other people, in this case, to know girls responsibly and well if I am to act justly toward them (Code, 1992, p. 89). Although I am aware of my position, I am mindful of what I can claim to know. I cannot presume to know. I have seen the girls over 3 years and continue to be in relation with them. I think about the knowledge claims made from seeing their visual narratives, not wanting to fall into what, perhaps, both researchers and teachers flatter themselves with:

Teachers flatter themselves that they have a deep knowledge of who their students are, until reality gives the lie to their belief. The greater the domination, the more dogmatic and doctrinaire the "knowledge" claimed, for the less it seeks information. In the same way, acknowledgment of the difficulty of understanding any "other" is an elementary mode of respect, a mode which moreover must imperatively be combined with a question about the way that the other perceives me, in other words with a recognition of reciprocity. (Le Dœuff, 1991, p. 74)

The girls were engaged in the cameraworks, and I sensed they were comfortable and that they enjoyed talking about and showing their photographs to me. Research relations, egalitarian and feminist, developed and changed with time in part due to my dual position of researcher and friend. My hope of reciprocity means my eye/i desires to see the girls as friends, next week, next month and 10 years from now. I worked to create a space for conversations, for the possibility to learn from understanding the evaded. I was hungry for a collective, an ability to move toward difference resulting from negotiated meaning between myself and the girls. How then do I, as Trinh Minh-Ha (1989) suggests, "inscribe difference without busting into a series of euphoric narcissistic accounts of yourself and your kind" (p. 28)? Acknowledging this I also found myself recognizing and learning how to work the hyphen of self and other with what Fine (1994b) suggests:

> Researchers probe how we are in relation with the contexts we study and with our informants, understanding that we are all multiple in those relations....I invite researchers to see how these "relations between" get us "better" data, limit what we feel free to say, expand our minds and constrict our mouths, engage us in intimacy and seduce us into complicity, make us quick to interpret and hesitant to write. Working the hyphen means creating occasions for researchers and informants to discuss what is, and is not, "happening between," within the negotiated relations of whose story is being told, why, to whom, with what interpretation, and whose story is being shadowed, why, for whom, and with what consequence. (p. 72)

Fidelity in research relationships is a "direct response to individuals with whom one is in relation" (Noddings, 1986, p. 497). I tried to be honest with myself and the girls in my narrative research as I worked to confirm and recognize genuine inquiry and reflection by nesting our work within an "ethic of caring" (Gilligan, 1982; Noddings, 1984). In regards to the use of photography, we employed a quality of "sensitivity" (Becker, 1974; Harper, 1987; Weiser, 1993), which lies at the centre of my relational work with the girls. Sensitivity requires that I work diligently to understand and develop an understanding of the girls' lives so that they may determine which individuals and activities may be photographed, in ways that are appropriate to do so, and how resulting images ought to be used (Gold, 1989, p. 103). As such, I see sensitivity rooted in the reciprocal nature, that of caring relationships between those engaged with this visual narrative inquiry.

# THE IMAGEMAKERS: CONSTRUCTING GIRLS' AGENCY

Who is taking the picture?
Who is doing the talking?
And if so by whom?

Oh, I thought I didn't have any reason, why not to have fun with this, with the camera it has the right to interrupt people's lives. (Morgan, Camerawork I)

But there's a kind of power thing about the camera. I mean everyone knows you've got some edge. You're carrying some slight magic which does something to them. It fixes them in a way. (Arbus, 1972, p. 13)

I had fun giving the girls cameras. I was curious, excited, and anxious to view their photographs. I wondered what images they would shoot? What they would pose for? Whose gaze was it anyway? I think a lot about what girls see:

Girls have till quite recently been relegated to a position of secondary interest, within both sociological accounts of subcultures and photographic studies of urban youth. The masculinist bias is still there in the subcultures themselves. Subject to stricter parent control than the boys, pinioned between the twin stigmas of being labeled "frigid" or a "slag", girls in subculture, especially working class culture, have traditionally been either silenced or made over in the image of the boys as replicas. (Hebdige, 1988, p. 27)

However, that tradition has been broken ever since riot grrls reshaped the meaning of girlhood. Our research group was named: "womyn and grrls in education." Our girlhood and educational experiences may not have been made of violence, tragedy and abuse, but sugar and spice? I see these girls' cameraworks as an interruption to the dominant image-flow and heterosexual survival and entitlement. These girls have not gone underground. Some of the girls' photographs are being shown and named, perhaps for the first time. They claim to be entitled to their bodies, schooling, careers and learn from seeing the sites of contest, knowing that girlhood transforms into womanhood. Greene (1993) reminds me, "Young people, perhaps especially, live on the surfaces, organize their lives by means of surfaces—choice, speed, chance—and the image systems that help make sense....Fast moving young people often wear masks, living among simulations that substitute things for other things" (p. 209).

## BETH

Beth, a Grade 10 student, attends an arts-based high school in western Canada. At 16, she tells and shows narratives about herself as a girl who loves her piano, making music, performing in drama productions and having relationships with friends. My relationship with Beth is intriguing. Initially, I felt discomfort with Beth, not really sure about how to take her. Beth plays with humor as a way to tell her stories, and with time, I learned from her use of humor. I consciously made our lives intersect with our love for music. I remember chats in my car and on the telephone and ones she asked to have "off the record." My reading of our conversations reveals how we scarcely spoke of school experiences in relation to the formal curriculum; stories of girls failing science, math, social studies are absent.

I taped our conversations; however, our second conversation of one and a half hours was missed. I forgot to press the record button. The following Phantom Interview is my telling of relooking at her "making metaphors" photographs after I drove her home:

### Phantom interview

I just "lost" an interview with Beth and missed an entire taped conversation. But are the recorded conversations the ones that count? I did not turn on the record button. I felt a comfort with Beth as we began by looking at her photographs, amazingly intimate spaces and stories about her bedroom. A visual narrative she pieced together with 5 photographs. It is through these photographs of her bedroom that she tells stories of popular advertising, stuffed animals, love of lights, an interior life that I see as incredible. Beth talks about the musicians she cares about: Great Deal, Tori Amos, X Series of Five. Tori Amos is a particular favorite. In another photograph, she turned the lens on herself, puts herself in the frame and chuckled when she looked at it. Perhaps it was not necessarily what she was anticipating. I see a face with a direct gaze, a youthful image, and a smile. I wondered how Beth might appear as a baby, and I thought about Beth as a little girl. I wondered how I would negotiate viewing her family photo albums with her. Her humor, her ability to tease me, breaks a tension and keeps the conversation going. The next picture she photographed her school locker, the inside door plastered with photographs of family: sisters, stepsister, her little godchild Sam, popular culture images, a picture of the Beatles and her friends. A telling image of Beth's daily life. Seeing her crutches leaning inside her locker left me wondering about living with cancer, of strength and silence. I evaded asking for stories. I avoided suggesting details or possible lead ins. Beth has a photograph of Maeve on the locker door, and she tells me about earlier girlhood memories of Waldorf schooling. Maeve is our connection to each other. I see her locker photograph layered with evaded experiences of hallway life. In her next photograph of ribbons, sweet grass and feathers, she speaks to her Cree heritage. This photograph opened a telling story of Beth's understanding of healing within her Cree history and her connections with her father who is an elder in the Native community. She told me about her father's role in her healing process after she went through her amputation. Then Beth tells me about living with her cancer at the age of 11. How do young girls make sense of dis-ease, cancer and amputation? Hard questions. I thought about who I was in this conversation with Beth telling me her painful stories. The next photograph is of a popular coffee house; she photographs her friends hanging out in the spaces where they like to sit. I wonder about the aesthetic pleasure of schools and how they lack comfortable home-like atmospheres. What do students look at? The next photograph taken by Maeve is a portrait of Beth sitting by her piano. Beth told me stories about her grandmother and the giving of the piano, which she loves. I think about what girls love. In a similar photograph Beth is sitting on her piano, these photographs provoked stories about making music and about Beth liking to sit on the top of her piano. In photograph Beth photographed her leg; perhaps this photograph provided a space, a possibility to objectify and see a separate part of her experience that integrates back into Beth's subjectivity of living with cancer. She told me stories of her phantom pain in relation to school experiences. Beth spoke of teachers' and students' difficulty in understanding and accepting phantom pain. The next shots are of her legs, and although Beth's leg is shown, it appears hidden by the illusion of a bent knee. I imagine what sense I can make of it, for now. Then in another photograph is her cat Licorice and stories of loving her cat. The next one is of the sunset as she is coming back from Christmas holidays and the sunrise and the sunset. The next picture is of her house, a mansion-like building in Toronto. Her father lives there with her sister and her stepmother. The next picture is of her at her stepsister's house on her nephew's swing, and she talks about swinging and its relation to gymnastics. I thought about the photographic work of Jo Spence (1995), in particular, a chapter called "The picture of health?" How does Beth make sense of what Spence writes about cancer and self-love. In the next photograph, Beth is standing in front of Einstein, the image is discolored; a red color disorients the image and I wonder how filters change ways of seeing. Her next shot is of her cat, which again speaks of her care for animals. This photograph is of her mother on the telephone. Beth seems to speak very highly of her mom and the place of the other three women in her life. In another photograph she was taking a picture of a girl from school in which she spoke of her junior high experiences and the difficulty she had in being thought of as an "odd" sort of individual. I cannot remember the exact words she used. She spoke about the boy who stuttered and a girl who has been bitten by a dog and of how the three of them were seen as outcasts. This story was followed by how much more she enjoyed the urban arts school. In another picture of the school hallway Beth spoke about the difficulty of sitting 75 minutes. I remember hating to sit that long when I was in high school. Beth also told stories about cutting out early. I remember that, too. What is a good length of time to sit on wooden chairs? The next photograph is from the bus stop, a familiar place, a daily life experience of arriving and leaving school. Bus stop stories. Her next photographs are of a drama production party, and she told stories about the cast from the play. I attended the performance, and I see faces that look familiar to me; there are photos of the entire cast, girls curling their hair, and flowers received after the "real" experience. Beth names all the girls, and I think about the relationship established. I have a sense that Beth knows a lot of people. In another photograph Beth is receiving a hug from a boy/man who I think is named Nathan, and she is wearing make-up, which she does not usually wear. She tells me stories about him being a close friend. The next photograph is of a young man who was in the lead role and in the dance. He also choreographed the last piece for the production. Beth says he is quite a talented guy. Photographs were shown of the party with friends laughing and drinking. The last photograph shows her "wonderful friend Tom," whom she has just met but had seen at the Fringe and repeatedly at various shows. Although she thought she would never see him again, ironically he attends the same high school and they meet formally on registration day. Since that time Beth and her friends named him Nathan. I sense Beth's desire to get to know Tom. Beth expresses her feelings for this boy and uses the words and a language to express her desire. She uses words foreign to me: "cheesy" is a favorite word, but I missed her exact words. I will ask her next time.

In writing this narrative introduction of Beth, of a missed conversation, I have attempted to frame my introduction to Maeve, Morgan and Thya in a similar way.

maeve—angel series

# MAEVE

Maeve is a Grade 11 student who attends an arts-based high school in western Canada. At 17 Maeve tells and shows narratives about herself as a girl who loves dancing, family and the body politic. My relationship with Maeve is one of ongoing friendship. Her siblings play with my daughter. Maeve speaks freely about figuring out friendships, desiring boyfriends and her struggles in becoming a woman. Maeve visits me frequently; we meet briefly at the doorstep and share conversation snips, highlights of friends and upcoming dance performances. My reading of our conversations reveals a frequency of how often we spoke of body and ballet.

When I began looking at Maeve's photographs, I saw spaces of warmth, friendship and love. I listened to her stories of growing up in a family nested within Rudolf Steiner philosophies of anthroposophy, leaving me intrigued with the place of Steiner's work in educational practices. I watch Maeve with curiosity and listen as she tells me about being a girl in relation to resisting womanhood. Her photographs show a fascination with re/presenting images of light and dark. Throughout her cameraworks, she has several photographs of lights, candles, and the dark. In her first photographs she showed images of the Holy Bible, with a back drop of white cotton fabric that I connect with her spirituality. She shows me parts of her bedroom, her desk at which she studies and draws, and personal artifacts, books and treasures. Maeve talks frequently about her mother for whom she cares deeply, her support and direction from her father, and her admiration of her younger brothers and sister.

Maeve was determined to recreate her ballet class photograph. A photograph of a photograph. This was a successful class, and she spoke about many positive dancing experiences with these girls. Stories of friendship and gossip flowed from this photograph. Yet, with each roll, Maeve wanted to capture it "better" than the time before. I became curious by Maeve's desire to recreate this already professional photograph. A photograph of a photograph. I thought a lot about this photograph as I read in various disciplines of understanding photographs mindful to what the girls and I negotiated at the beginning of the research. I am listening to stories about their photographs. I listen to what Maeve thought about ballet relationships, competition, and response to success. Maeve spends hours at the ballet school with girls and women. Maeve talks about her desire to be a dancer, "really, really wanting to be a dancer" and of "teaching children." Maeve has spent past summers working as a camp leader at a nearby historical site where she enacted a persona of the big sister or mother.

She tells stories about the dance politics of this place as she makes sense of what she sees and hears. I sense Maeve trying to integrate the contradictions of home and ballet life: the personal and the private. I feel a direct connection with Maeve as I remember similar stories from other subculture politics: direct contradiction between values and beliefs at home and the outside public. Sites of contests that press for different ways to see. I appreciate Maeve's intensity and her ability to search and to ask questions through sustained conversation.

The next photo-narrative that moved me was her photographs of her body: a mini-narrative about the body politic of ballet dancing. She photographed: her toes pressed up against her white dresser; her knees; a head shot; face shot; the back of her head with a ballet bun; her hand with her fingers spread out wide with rings and a watch; her backside sitting in a chair; another bending over; a chest shot; a stomach shot; her feet; bare toes; work socks; and one of her pointe shoes next to a book about Karen Kain. The series continues with photographs of getting ready, performing feminine rituals, hair, teeth, body and a weigh scale. Seeing her photographs made me think of Haug's (1987) body memory work in female sexualization.

She also shows photographs of herself sleeping. Seeing her sleeping pressed another way of seeing Maeve. I am curious about girls' dreams, desires and hopes as I reflect on the girls in my Master's work (Bach, 1993) and see how their lives change as they challenge traditional scripts of being a woman. I wonder how girls negotiate the contradictions of the larger culture. What is protected from them? What is told? This photograph opened a telling story of ballet and cultural expectations of having the right body for ballet. Maeve spoke to Canadian and Russian expectations. I am impressed with her critique as she begins to accept her body, as she re-invents her self with her body. How do young girls make sense of the body in their homes, in relation to other symbols and images? It is a hard question to understand. I thought about who I was in this conversation with Maeve, telling body stories of eating and not eating, and I remembered my own stories.

Her next photographs were taken by her younger brother: they show a photo-narrative of 10 fashion photographs that Maeve imagines. I see them as a kind of angel series. Here in a purple blue long dress Maeve stands, sits, lies on a snow-covered ground. Her hands and toes are in ballet position as she poses in positions from hanging in a tree, doing the splits, dancing and burying her hands and feet in the snow: strong images of beauty for Maeve. Hearing Maeve's enthusiasm for a different look for fashion magazines makes me think about who is creating the image? The signified? And what is seen? Listening to Maeve's stories and seeing her photographs has been a learning experience for me as I learn to see in the light and write stories of a friend.

## MORGAN

Morgan is a school friend of Maeve's and Beth's and attends the same arts-based high school. At 16, she tells and shows narratives about home, school, and friends. Her stories are about time spent alone and times when she is in relation with others. She cares for her family and speaks about her mother and her younger sister and brother openly. She tells stories about sustained conversation as she and her mother reflect on authoring different lives that fit with their values of family. Morgan reads philosophy while she questions authorities and the overarching power relations as she writes her life. I shared some of my books about girls' writing and psychological development with her, while she suggested ones that I might enjoy. Morgan keeps me on my toes. I am comfortable in my relation with Morgan, and regardless of time lapses, we seem to pick up our conversations where we left off.

I write about Morgan's life intersecting with learning from strangers and learning as coming home. Morgan tells me that she learns from her mother's lived experiences and how she and her family negotiate the place of institutional authority. Morgan speaks about her understanding of evaded stories, sexuality, smoking, relationships and has an ability to move beyond difference and make connections with her public and personal life. I see Morgan as a serious and sincere girl. Her questioning and thinking presses me to think about what it means to be an educated girl. Morgan has a strength of self that I see as different from other girls with whom I speak.

I was attentive to my research entry with Morgan. Morgan asked questions about the place of photography in research and the ethics of visual research, as did Morgan's mother. I learned from her to title my "media release" as an "academic release" (see Appendix C). Morgan expressed a desire to be part of my research to Maeve. As a researcher I was pleased. I remember people asking, "How will you get participants?" In our first telephone call, I can still hear Morgan's easeful voice telling of her involvement in the visual arts, about loving photography, and I sensed her desire to be a part of the work. Morgan questioned the criteria for my research, Did she need a camera? film? I hoped by telling her I would be purchasing the cameras and film and developing the film that my frame for this research was okay for her. I wanted high school girls who actively connected their learning to the arts.

We first meet at a cafe in her neighborhood. We shared some food as we talked about the camerawork, and I showed her Judy Weiser's book to give her an idea about my thoughts on photography. Morgan's questions regarding the use of cameras and about getting the "right," the "perfect" photograph, pressed me to think about how I engage the girls to be part of the visual narrative work. What entices? Why would girls participate? Who gains?

Morgan photographed her daily life with intensity and determination. A mind like a camera is full of ideas, and long after the cameraworks were completed, Morgan continued to document her world visually. We still have three rolls of film to talk about from her visit to Japan with a school exchange. Morgan made me think about how honest I am to myself and to others. I found a lost part of myself with Morgan, and her awakeness to family roots made my story clearer.

## THYA

Thya, a Grade 11 student, attends a large academic urban high school in western Canada. At 17, Thya tells and shows narratives about herself as a girl who loves ballet dancing, her boyfriend and girlfriends. My relationship with Thya seems to shadow my high school stories that span over age, generation, and social class categories. I see our lives intersecting with our search for relations with men. Thya's early and desperate struggle for understanding personal relations with young men is traced though compulsory stories of being a heterosexual girl. Thya speaks about entitlement with body and tells stories that have enabled me to go back and look at my high school memories. Our conversations move toward personal conversations and end with wonders about Thya's ability to analyze authorities in positions in power:

Sometimes I think of school and I just get like horrible feelings. I just can't wait to get out. Sometimes school makes me feel really sad and lonely for some reason. I don't know why. The only reason I go is because of my friends. I love it because I see my friends. The odd teacher I like, and the odd class I enjoy. It's just something, it's just a feeling of dying to get out. A few days ago I felt so sick, I didn't feel like going to school. Then I thought my boyfriend's going to be there and I know he'll bring me a treat.

Thya's daily school life echoes stories and images from my high school life of 20 years ago. She tells stories of wanting to escape from school, stories of alienation, of boredom and oppressive school rules. Hearing fragments of Thya's school and daily life stories makes me attentive to the reproduction of the evaded curriculum. What stories do girls tell about school and to whom?

Thya's photographs are mini-narratives of parties with friends, boyfriends and family celebrations. Thya repeats these visual narratives through the cameraworks. Her first narrative raised ethical dilemmas in re/presenting the making of girl culture (see "An example," page 67).

One narrative was about Christmas Eve, and Thya told stories about her family traditions and stories of her sister's marriage, her nieces, and her younger sister. Looking at photographs of her mother, Thya tells stories about her mother's relationship with her father; on photographs of her niece, Thya speaks to her sister's long-time marriage, a relationship that works, one that is "loving," "good" and "caring." Thya values marriage and romantic love and learns from what she is seeing as she looks at her grandmother's marriage, her mother's marriage, and her sister's marriage. I hear her attempting to make sense of the heterosexual relationships in/through/against other. We talked a lot about marriage.

## MAKING THE PRIVATE PUBLIC

the girls produced photographs
mirrored within private/public production
stories of the body
basically private, intimate experiences
but also made public
for other
knowledge
other people's stories
what re/presents knowledge
both realized and evaded
how can
i
grow
without losing
or becoming
alien

In *Public bodies—Private sates*, Brettle and Rice (1994) acknowledge the boundaries of public and private, and their convergence in the site of the body are at once suggested, located and problematized:

The body is a highly contested site—its flesh is both the recipient and source of desire, lust and hatred. As a pawn of technology, it's sacred and sacrificial, bearing the politics of society and state. The body is our common bond, yet it separates us in its public display of identity, race and gender. (Augaitis, cited in Ewing, 1994, p. 324)

There is debate about girls, and discourse continues around the pleasure and danger of the body. It is my hope to reframe possibilities of seeing and listening to girls. How to decide which words and which photographs, at once suggested and located, problematized my ideas of private. Each photograph shown opens a dialogue with those who look at them.

You don't have to worry about saying that on the transcript. I mean until it becomes public. This is my big debate, what is private for me may not be the same thing for you. Who you talk to and show your photographs is up to you. I mean I'm not going to show your mom the transcripts. We'll decide together what will be public. My work is with you [the girls].

*I feel responsible for words I make public.*

*What happens when we make girls' photographs public?*

**Fine.**

*What's at risk?*
*for the girls*
*for me*
*for others*

I'm not going to show anything without you knowing.

*What is life without risk?*

**Okay, but I can show my mom if I want to.**

*I continue to let the girls know what I make public.*

*others*

for sure
that's great

*Who will the girls show their photographs to?*
*What stories will they make public?*
*What is my responsibility in making the girls' photographs public?*

The distinction between public and private, perhaps, the dated slogan of "the personal is political" lingers in my mind as I see the implications of this distinction working against girls. The artificial division between the public and private means analyzes are needed to investigate how "the division was created and constantly reinvigorated, what work it does, and why it was seductive when daily life is so often ignored or rejected it.…Public/private is one such metaphor" (Jordanova, 1994, cited in Brettle & Rice, 1994, p. viii). One way I imagine the relationship between the personal and public is to imagine a fine line between the two spheres. I can imagine the personal pleasure on one side and the public danger on the other. Blurring, pulling or erasing the fine line between the private-public writing on the body makes possible a space for sharing stories to frame questions about evaded stories in the girls' lives. Alcoff and Gray (1993) address the need for new ways to analyze the personal and the political as well as new ways to conceptualize these terms:

> Experience is not "pretheoretical" nor is theory separate or separable from experience, and both are always already political. A project of social change, therefore, does not need to "get beyond" the personal narrative or the confessional to become political but rather needs to analyze the various effects of the confessional in different contexts and struggle to create discursive spaces in which we can maximize its disruptive effects. (pp. 283–284)

What can be said about photography in a patriarchal order that privileges vision over other senses? Can I not expect them to be a domain of masculine privilege? Working with the girls and their photographs and stories emphasizes the artistry that shapes my vision. My interpretations are positioned by that past: "That a point of view can be understood as both the experienced 'I', and the 'eye' which 'looks out' and optically defines the public space has ramifications unique to photography and other photo-related media within visual arts" (Brettle & Rice, 1994, p. 30).

morgan—talking out of both sides of your mouth

## PHOTOGRAPH ETHICS: TALKING OUT OF BOTH SIDES OF YOUR MOUTH

With respect to the use of photography I employ a quality of "sensitivity" (Becker, 1974; Harper, 1987; Weiser, 1993), which lies at the centre of my relation with participants. Sensitivity requires that I work diligently against "othering" by attempting to understand their lives so that they may determine which individuals and activities to photograph and how resulting images ought to be used (Gold, 1989, p. 103). As such, I see sensitivity rooted in the reciprocal nature: that of caring relations among those engaged with visual narrative inquiry, the reciprocity and caring relationships that I explored in the section "Research relationships" in this notebook. I am mindful to a "covenantal ethic" (Gold, 1989) as a way to negotiate relations between those who tell and visually show life stories and share personal experiences.

Morgan (94-12-02)
Cameraworks I
Projective photographs

Okay, how did you take this picture?

*how will I locate those people?*

Oh yeah! But I don't talk to them.
Because I really didn't know them.
I'm sure they have forgotten I took
their picture.                          *who forgets?*
I thought it was quite fun. That day    *exploitation*
I was a very energetic person, so I     *using*
had the courage to go up and ask.       *othering*

It does take courage doesn't it?        *being a photographer changes my position*

                                        *and it is a different tool...*
                                        *and any tool can be used and abused*

And then this is where I lost the       *lost...*
camera at the bowling alley.            *what happens with lost film?*

Okay

*Okay*
*Is it okay? I think hard about why I am*
*okay.*

Who owns the image? the negative?
Are the photographs the researcher's? for how long?
What was negotiated in the research ethics?
Who can be shown the photographs?
What about others in the photographs?
With digital imaging, I find myself asking another question. Instead of asking questions about informed consent, I find myself asking questions about "epistemic responsibility" (Code, 1987) in relation to the camera-works, and I attempt to show how the ethics of visual narratives are like talk-ing out of both sides of your mouth. I cannot find a standpoint that con-cludes that a given image is a true record of a real scene or event. We can take the opposite tack and attempt to demonstrate that it could not be a true record (Mitchell, 1992, p. 30). This example of listening to Morgan speak about three photographs provides an appropriate and effective theoretical point of making sense of photographic ethics—of how I inevitably talk out of both sides of my mouth. Together we negotiated which photographs would and would not be shown

Morgan (94-12-02)
Camerawork 1                         *what am I asking?*
Projective project                   *what's my intention?*

PHOTOGRAPH ONE               *producing by projecting*

This is a picture of my two friends.
I think this is the first one I took.
I didn't know what to take
a picture of.                        *what does she think I want?*
Tattoos,                             *I listen and hope I haven't limited*
a kind of big thing in our little    *Morgan.*
group.
I mean we all like tattoos,
but I never had it done.
She's got one,
and she is a rebel.                  *rebel*
                                     *How do girls name themselves?*
                                     *each other?*

an animal rights protester
by pretending

*Are these photographs real?*
*staged? posed?*
*what is re/presented*
*with light?*

they're lesbians.

*identity*
*the body*
*sexuality*
*gender questions*
*relationships*

This girl here she just sat down
put her arm around her
and smiled as if they were
lovers.

*love*
*Western notions of romantic love*
*girls showing affection*
*to each other*
*lesbians*
*I think of compulsory scripts of hetero-*
*sexuality.*

## PHOTOGRAPH TWO

This has got to be the weirdest person.

*weirdest*
*how do girls*
*construct identities?*
*name themselves within patriarchal*
*culture?*

I know.

*how do we know?*
*who knows*
*knowledge as othering?*

She is really out of this world.
She loves to just act.
She is in drama.

*a space that allows for the weird,*
*the bizarre.*

Here she is just making the
weirdest face,
just being herself.

*being herself*
*how does a girl sustain being*
*herself at the*
*crossroads?*

We have a lot in common.
We both like Janice Joplin.

*I listen to Janice Joplin sing of love*
*hearing generations of her music*
*reproduced in our daily lives.*

We recite all the words to her songs
while we are waiting for the bus
and we sing.

*singing as a way*
*being heard*
*voice*

And would you give her that picture?  *photo-sorting*
*giving what a researcher wants*

If she wanted it,
but I would like to keep it.  *photo-gathering*

I would make doubles you know.  *sharing in a collaborative relationship*

## PHOTOGRAPH THREE

I didn't even know these two girls,  *photo-taking*
but I thought just to start out
when you're asking for
something
that is different.
I thought that the fact she
has green dyed hair
I thought I'd politely ask,
and they had no problem with it.

*making the camera visible*
*being mindful to other*
*reminding*

It was one of the ethical things you  *What is remembered?*
talked about, remember.  *What is memory?*

When I said you left me with a
heavy issue thinking of the
the ethics of using the camera

photographing people, things, life
I said
ask straight out *fine*
and then you're fine. *What is epistemic responsibility in
photo-taking?*

**These two girls didn't want to
have their faces shown.**
**if you were going to show their** *Who will read*
**tattoos** *see
them in the research?*
They weren't quite sure what was *concern and wonder*
done with the photograph. *How can I ever know what is done
with our photographs, digital pho-
tographs?
photocopies
CNN nasty people*

**would be used for** *researcher's dilemma, for me at least
used/abused*
They didn't want their faces to be *voyeur*
shown *exploitation*

**Since she lives with her Grand-** *what's seen?*
**mother** *by whom?
What's hiding?*
**I don't even think her Grandmother** *not seen*
**knows she had that** *What's marked?*
tattoo.

**Tattoos** *body marking*
**So I thought I really don't know, but** *beauty*

But again I mean by the time the
book comes we can negotiate. *negotiate*
Because I don't know what pictures *determining what's in and*
will be in the book, I don't know yet *what's out*
what you know is we won't know until
we've gone through the entire project. *photo-taking
photo-gathering
photo-viewing*

Sure, and she was eager
this girl was sure and she was so
eager to
have her picture taken
she's into the camera.                  *desiring being pictured*

See she does
she just likes making faces
making people laugh.                    *laughing and pleasure*
                                        *I think of laughing and crying.*

I have noticed that a lot of your photographs are of people pictured
making direct contact.

                                        *Who do we aim our gaze at and why?*
                                        *Who's taking the picture?*
Oh, yeah.                               *Who is looking?*

To you then that makes sense, that
you would have asked them permis-       *care*
sion and they didn't know that at the   *responsibility*
time.

I found it.
                                        *I hope*
It makes sense.
                                        *the body feeling*
Its hard not to because I'm not good
at just taking.
I felt too guilty.                      *guilty*
and they know when I take a picture
and then don't they see me again
I don't know they might hunt me         *culpable, fault, error*
down                                    *sentenced*
                                        *awful.....Judy Weiser helped me make*
but I don't know.                       *sense of this.*
But if...it's an incident
that I see that looks neat              *thinking about*
lately it's like I've got more ideas and *healthy photo-taking*
with a flash                            *photo-viewing*
it's working great.                     *photo-gathering*

With regards to my visual research, I take seriously the words of May (1977, 1980), who advocates the covenant as a way of being between researcher and participants because "the covenantal relationship is primary; it involves neither subjects nor objects, but human beings" (May, cited in Gold, 1989, p. 105). I see the girls writing their lives, authoring stories and creating images of their daily lives. There is risk in our visual work. Knowing who I am in relation to the girls and their cameraworks means I attend to what May (1980) writes about a covenantal ethic, that is, "at the heart of a covenant is an exchange of promises, an agreement that shapes the future between two parties. This promise grows…and acknowledges the other.…It emphasizes gratitude, fidelity, even devotion, and care" (p. 367). I am mindful about how I negotiate relations between the girls who tell stories and share personal experiences about their photographs. As a visual narrative researcher, caring, sensitivity and covenantal ethics are related. I cannot be engaged in the reciprocal relationship required by the covenant without engaging myself in/with hearing and understanding the girls' lived experiences, beliefs, values, and views of their worlds. The covenantal ethic cues me to deliberate the girls' needs in my researching and publishing (Gold, 1989, p. 105).

I have been attentive to the unique dilemmas that arise from employing visual methods. I believe that the application of sensitivity grounded in covenantal ethics provides insight and understanding made available using photography within narrative methodology without harming the girls and/or myself. Working within a framework of care enhances the research relationship by encouraging me to stay aware of the girls' understandings of what is included in the visual narrative research process. However, no code, outlook, or technique ensures that ethical problems will be resolved. "Covenant ethics is responsive in character" (May, 1977, p. 69), and consequently, I remain ready to alter or abandon the use of visual re/presentation if I have good reason to believe that the girls are being adversely affected (Gold, 1989; May, 1977, 1980; Weiser, personal communication, February 20–23, 1994).

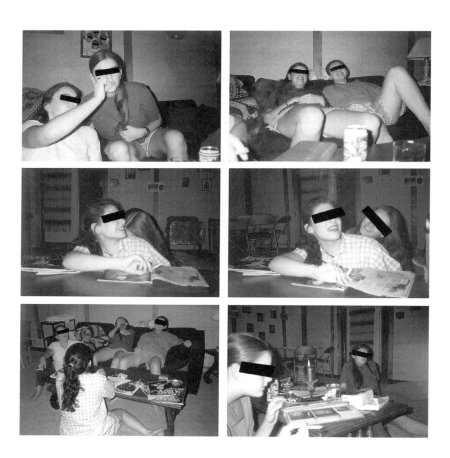

*thya—an example*

## AN EXAMPLE

"See."

"Look."

"Oh my, what are they doing?"

"My daughter would never do that!"

"You can't ethically show that."

"Who blacked out their eyes?"

Over the last 3 years of exhibiting girls' photographs, I have encountered viewers' responses that place me within ethical positions of needing to acknowledge the response after listening to what others had to say. How can I respond to ignorant, even naive/moralistic commentaries about these photographs? How can there be conversation around the silence? the illegal? the private?

Herein lies an ethical dilemma of being a researcher as I learn to respond while making the private public. What is that? What is never? What are they doing? What is seen? I was intrigued by this photo-narrative Thya created but not without troubling my responsibility of being a researcher. When I see Thya's photographs, I understand her stories to be a part of the evaded curriculum, and from the onset of my project, my intention has been to uncover/reveal aspects of the evaded curriculum. Yet, somehow, showing this particular photograph of girls smoking pot has troubled my ethical responsibility in re/presenting girls' lives. As some have reminded me, marijuana use is illegal, and I wonder is the evaded also illegal, or is the illegal very often evaded? Making the private public has been a contentious issue for me from the beginning. I was faced with the irony of re-encapsulating the evaded by realizing that knowing the coded indexical nature of reading photographs there are some I did not wish to show. The further irony is that by maintaining that position I call into question the intentionality of my research. In discussions with the girls, we were prepared to take the risk and make the private public.

I remember seeing this photograph the first time; it is one in a series from a photo-narrative of seven photographs. Did this photograph please me? Interest me? Intrigue me? Perhaps. There is nothing extraordinary in it. The photograph has the banality of a party atmosphere: two girls sharing a joint with a beer can off to the right. However, my gaze is pulled to the framed family photograph hanging directly above the girls. I was sure this photograph existed for me; it is a silhouette from my life stories and presses me to look. The attraction for this photograph has been the question of response to the evaded in girls' lives.

What matters is what Thya tells: "I want teachers to know that all the girls at our school smoke pot, even if they don't want to believe it." What is one to think seeing girls toking and drinking? I hear the echoes of bad girl stories. Good girls just don't do those things? Too awful to think about. As a researcher I think about the stories told around the photo-narrative Thya has created. What were her expectations? What was she trying to tell me and others? What was she wanting us to see? What is taught and learned by showing a photograph with girls smoking marijuana and drinking?

**Thya (95-01-04)**
**Camerawork 1**
**Projective photographs**

Okay, the parents peeking in.

*As Bateson (1994) tells us,* "Trying to improve people by interfering with their own preferences often makes things worse. One of the behaviors that is most easily condemned in other communities is drug use, although chemical tinkering with mental states is very nearly a human universal. Almost all human groups have found something to eat or drink, to sniff or smoke, that alters moods even metaphysics, but these practices are less dangerous when suppressed. It is often custom, not chemistry, that determines whether a practice is harmful, and many interferences disrupt custom and leave chemistry to do its worst" (p. 219).

Isn't that hilarious, and there's Belinda as a little tiny kid. And her brother

*I think of family photo albums but also who sees this photograph. Wonders about the photo-viewing.*

Wouldn't her parents just die.

*my motherhood card emerges*

I think so. Yeah, makes it tough. But that was so fun; I mean, even there she is reminiscing, she was showing us pictures of her dad and stuff.

*I'm curious to hear Thya tell this story.*

Okay,

And is this night just with girls?

Yeah, just girls. That's Madeline, she is more of an acquaintance. I don't really know her that well. But she's good friends with my good friend Belinda.

*acquaintance/friend*

Yeah.

So that was the funnest night because that was one night right after school started in September. Sometime after when I talked to you. Forget when I talked to you but.

*what is fun?*

*I first spoke to Thya in September 1995.*

Really in September.

That was sometime right after the long weekend,

when the school year was starting.

One quick party before school started. It was just a couple of us. She's got long, long hair.

*My eye catches the images of the girls.*

Oh, doesn't she, well it's short now. Oh it was such beautiful hair. But it was so nice. Okay, we only had

like two beers that night. There was
four of us. Well, actually two beer
and I think 26 of Vodka; we didn't
really think about it. Well we did a
little bit. She had one glass of it and
she threw up.

Oh, really.

Like one little drink, I don't how she
got, but that's kind of like me.

On a empty stomach, maybe too
much.

*I speak from experience. What did Thya
hear? Somehow I feel I am a silhouette.
I have no fear for her. But how do I
give of myself to her?*

But that was weird because Emma
never smoked. But she did when we
were alone. She'll have a cigarette in
her mouth, but she never inhales. I
don't think she's ever inhaled a cigarette.

*Oh right, "never inhale." I doubt.*

She'll just leave them hanging in her
mouth.

Yeah, and then just blow it out. And
she pretends to be Marilyn Monroe.
I have fun with it, too. I haven't
done it in a while. I hate smoking, I
find it is very disgusting habit. But it
is fun sometimes when I am just
with my girlfriends and we pretend
we smoke. While actually she
smokes, really, really hard she
smokes about a pack a day about.

*pretending to be*

*I see many girls smoking in and out of
school.*

Oh, wow.

But the rest of my friends don't
smoke.

I would smoke, too, mainly when we drank or we were at a party, it seems like.

*It was a look.*

See, that's what I mean. To look cool with your friends.

I used to do that, yeah.

But I don't do that for some reason. I don't know, all my friends do but

*It happens? chapter on why girls smoke.*

Then they are having a good laugh.

That was always after, we were laughing and

And is this just girls?

*Girls Grrls*

Yeah, just girls.

*I know it's different when the boys are around.*

Okay.

We have to do that sometimes; we all get together and we would drink. You know, I don't drink when I'm with my boyfriend because I don't know. It's not fun drinking with your boyfriend. The whole fun of drinking is when you're with a group of people. It's to flirt with guys and not really feel so bad about it. Like I mean just flirt, I don't know. But you know what, it was just awful, we went to a New Years Eve party, and she is so awful. I just set her up with one of my good friends, Eric. He's this really good looking motor bike guy from my school; he is only in my

*I know/I don't know.*

*not feeling bad.*

*I remember my boyfriend's dirt bikes. I had a lot of fun dirt biking, although I know my parents worried about me.*

grade. But he is a really sweet guy. On New Years Eve, we went out to my friend's cabin, you know its the best thing to do, if you want a party. No one leaves. You just crash for the night. And we drank, but I couldn't drink; I threw up, I don't know why. I only had I think I had a beer and a half and one vodka drink. Which isn't that much and it was over a long time. But I saw other people threw up, and the party started getting out of hand kind of. Just too many people showed up, and it ended up being a cool party, and all these university guys from Vancouver that were back visiting their parents like the biker, a rich guy. They had their Jeeps and bikes, they all showed up. Very, very sleazy and lots of them were very horny, you know. Like all of sudden they would pick everyone up. But not really succeeding be-cause there was so many people. That you just couldn't pay attention, and all the other girls were so drunk. And she, she kissed Eric, and you would think they were going out. Then she passed out on this bed, threw up and passed out, and was pretending to kiss another guy. And he just told me today what she did. So I was so upset with her, she really betrayed me because I told her that she really, really likes Eric. And she asked me if I could have them both over at my house and we would hang out and rent movies. So we did that, and she has this charm and I knew it would work and it did. Now she has him, and the chase is over.

*sweet guy…honorable men…*

*I nod agreeing it is a good thing to do.*

*drinking and driving*
*I think about drinking and driving- media images of "bloody idiots" and "just say no."…I think about how people continue to get into cars with drunk drivers?*
*Is there a way to drink responsibly? Who teaches us?*

*Sleazy…horny…you know*
*I know…and I think about stories that are silent and silenced about sexual arousal. Do we teach alternatives to intercourse?*

*What is seen as betrayal? bad/good?*

That's what she figures, she's that
kind of a girl. You know those girls. *that kind of girl?*

You say the chase. *chasing and flirting...who is doing*
 *what?*

Yeah.

Yeah, a lot of girls do that?

Yeah, she's very bad for that. And I
thought this time she wouldn't just
because she said it was about time
she needs a boyfriend. *needs a boyfriend...*

Yeah, thinks.

Yeah, thinks she needs a boyfriend. I
haven't even talked to her. Called
her twice before I came over because
I was at Eric's house. And I really

He was really upset by this.

Yeah, he goes "I'm choked"; that's a
very guy thing to do, I think.

And he even said that? *I wonder how we talk about our feel-*
 *ings......My doubt relates to my limited*
A very guy thing to do and he, you *trust.*
know. I don't know about that; I
don't usually hear about girls doing
it. So I'm upset with her; she broke
my trust. *Trust. Who do we trust?*

So are you going to talk to her.

Oh yeah, I just going to like, maybe she'll explain. Because Brenda, one of his friends Dave saw this happen. Supposedly Eric was right beside her on the bed passed out. There was lots of drinking that night. So many rich teenagers.

Who's cabin was this out at.

Jack's place, Michelle's friend, Jack. I mean I'm sad kind of about it. We all had permission; my mom even drove me up. I told her that there would be drinking.

That's just incredible.

Yeah, isn't she great. My mom is great, like I said I called her up at night and said, "Mom they're all too drunk to drive. One guy puked on my sleeping bag, so I want to go can you please come and get me." And she goes no, is your life in danger, I say no. And she goes then forget it, I drove you up there, I'm tired, and I'm going to bed. So she wouldn't come and get me; she trusts me, you know. She knows I'm not going to do anything stupid.

NO. What do you mean about something stupid. What does that mean?

It's hard to say because I drank, and I know I didn't do anything stupid.

Like you would go out and

*What do girls tell their mothers? Are they silent or telling or retelling.*

*danger/pleasure?*

*I remember my parents saying, "Don't do anything stupid." Who decides what's stupid? Is it only stupid if it's illegal?*

Fool around with some guy.

Okay.

That's what I mean about stupid.

Okay, so mother doesn't believe that you're intimate with Dana.

*A one night stand is stupid.... Who says.*

No, oh no.

Okay.

*I doubt...a little.*

Well, I don't know. It's hard to say because sometimes she's crazy, like she'll let me go in my room with him, for hours. And we won't be doing something all the time. But I mean she won't interrupt and then we'll

Doesn't she know, I mean she must know.

*What can we presume to know?*

She will never ask me; I know her enough.

*What is not addressed/acknowledged in families?*
*Why are we still silent about sexual practices?*
*Why are we continuing a practice of moral fear?*
*When do we talk about pleasure?*

No, this is the same picture.

You're looking at magazines. What magazines are you reading?
This one's called *Seventeen*.

*I remember reading* Seventeen.

# Notebook 3

In my writing relationship, I found inroads, insights and intrusions layering my analysis of learning from photographs and stories through/against/with cultural scripts acting to define girlhood culture in an already interpreted world. In composing this visual research method, the personal became clearer bit by bit, in ways I had not anticipated. Learning from seeing has challenged me and called into question self and the evaded in relation to the writing on the body of girls.

I write about what is seen. I suggest that experience is constructed through blending in the confusion between who produces meaning and who consumes meaning. The complicity in the writing provokes questions about the constitution of subjectivity through a range of strategies. The effort of each girl's contribution has been organic and rewarding. I feel these writings and visual narratives extend contemporary thought about curriculum, particularly in directions that ensure a more interdisciplinary and photographic and poetic approach and cross over into areas that reflect postmodern practices of theoretical discussion and scholarship. In this notebook, I weave a rich history of feminist thought and writing, educational theory, and the postmodern crisis of representation as I continue the debate, theorizing and critiquing the representation prevalent to narrative research. Here I wish to ask of my reflection and supposedly telling stories what photographs get shown, how and why? This is my way of writing a research text, a composition of seeing the photographs and hearing the stories.

After months of contemplation, discussion, presenting and writing, I have produced a text that works to challenge commonly held definitions of girls and knowledge claims made with/against/through them. As a researcher in relation with high school girls I found myself yearning for an "us," a desire to close any possible distance between "me and them" to what Fine and Macpherson (1995) write about as they listen to struggles for sameness while negotiating territories of race, gender, class and difference. Together they trace a discourse of power and difference in a conversational territory that calls me to think about a "hungry for an us" (p. 4).

beth
maeve
morgan
thya

how do i start
i know that we have already started
so maybe i'm asking how to continue
what do i tell
show
and leave
why can't i make sense of this.....again
what's the meaning?

i want to share your stories
but i continue
to worry/trouble how your narratives will be read
and seen
in an already interpreted world
how might i show and tell with a
difference
a way that will change
how we listen to girls
of how you see your worlds

i think of the man who tells a
'bimbett' story
naming girls, objectifying, using, abusing
words echo in my mind
in my body
of being seen

what is missed? dismissed?
makes me wary
uncertain
will girls' visual narratives
change/transform/inform policy
make a difference to the curriculum
in/out of school?

or will we continue to
evade/avoid/dodge/escape from
shun and sidestep
or acknowledge
approach
clarify/confess/confront/confirm
declare
elucidate
encounter
explain
expound
face
illustrate
meet
prove

girls'
experience or
evade
elude
baffle
equivocate

i know i have much to say
but often
i feel blocked
silenced
in my position
when i feel
in my body the emotions
embodied
that swirl through

up and down
some that stay hidden
denial
what are you saying hedy?

argue
you need an argument

i don't want to
what am i arguing for
i am necessarily troubled
to argue/command/dictate
it means winners and losers
it means exclusion
because of position i might
ignore overlook propound
or i could discuss
plead
dispute
differ
talk about
hold/harmonize

can i hold a narrative
a visual narrative to
illustrate
make more human
the personal/political
by
putting a face to the word
putting a picture to the story
show not just tell
but talk about girls' lives
a body
a some body
who is busy living a life
in an already interpreted world

# I SEE, I AM NOT SEEN

The only thing that is different from one time to another is what is seen. (Stein, 1926)

I catch my eye to evoke memories. I look to connect stories simply because no photograph I see contains as much visual information as the story might actually disclose. As a photographer, I know the girls and I cannot depict everything we see. Therefore, the only thing that is different from one time to the next are the stories told around the photo-taking, photo-viewing and photo-gathering from the girls' cameraworks. As a researcher working with girls, I question: What is seen? Whose look matters? Whose gaze is met? Which look is universalized?

Investment in the look is not as privileged in women as in men. More than other senses, the eye objectifies and masters. It sets at a distance, and maintains a distance. In our culture the predominance of the look over smell, taste, touch and hearing has brought about an impoverishment of bodily relations. The moment the look dominates, the body loses its materiality. (Irigaray, cited in Pollock, 1988)

The eye/i that dominates. The eye/i that resists. What is lost?
I believe seeing is learning. I am attempting to write about (looking) as a way to disrupt the taken-for-granted of what is seen in an already interpreted world:

But for us the world becomes most densely informative, most luscious, when we take it in through our eyes. It may even be that abstract thinking evolved from our eye's elaborate struggle to make sense of what they saw. Seventy percent of the body's sense receptors cluster in the eyes, and it is mainly through seeing the world that we appraise and understand it. (Ackerman, 1990, p. 230)

So what is seen? What happens in girls' lives when shadows that disrupt categories of knowing and are sites for understanding the unfamiliar are not seen by those who author girls' experiences? A reviewer of Oliver Sacks' (1997) latest text, *The island of the color blind*, tells of Sacks' research with children on the island of Pingelap:

There are laughing children in the sunlight but in shadows are children with achromatopsia, their heads covered, or their eyes squinting to avoid the brightness. Many islanders carry a recessive gene for the condition they call makum (literally, not see) others are affected by total color blindness. The principal symptoms are the intolerance to bright light and inability to see fine detail. (MacGregor, 1997, p. D16)

What happens when we no longer look in the shadows? What happens when we do not see girls' experiences? I think about my ability to see the unfamiliar, the concealment of other. I turn my gaze, drop my eyes to avoid the brightness, and I share this ability with the blind. I think about color blindness and how a person's eyeglasses do not help me to observe the rules, and I am not clear what part my eye plays in seeing how to solve a problem. To hide and evade girls' experiences is, in my view, a Thou shalt not see discourse, which serves only to maintain a sort of blindness that marks the (dialogues) between author-researcher and the authored—the girl. I am interested in my ability to see as it contrasts with incapacities of color/moral blindness, and I know that not everything I say about what I see is relevant. What is seen if blinders are removed? What reinforces society's blindness?

Has "normal" vision limited what we see? I think about multiple ways of seeing and about spaces created for girls to pursue "separate visions" (Bateson, 1994, p. 15). I think about the images that linger in my mind, a double vision of past experiences, haunting images that create discomfort on my body and press my search for triple vision. What happens when indexical sanctioned codes of seeing continue to institutionally ignore, dismiss, distort and misrepresent what girls show and tell us. Barthes (1981) argues that the photograph's value as evidence is seared into it by its indexical nature. It is something that was institutionally and historically produced; it has to be argued for. Otherwise,

the photographs are just bits of chemically discolored paper or, more to the point in this case, just bits of postcards. Seeing a photograph as somehow having the clout of truth is something that has to be produced, argued for, institutionalized...the trace of a historical gaze; uncover, perhaps, the way that gaze was engineered and institutionally sanctioned, so that looking became caught up in the idea of the truth of the photograph and its evidential weight. (p. 69)

I want to talk about photographs' evidential value as something that is contestable and, in fact, contested. What happens if we turn our photographic gaze upon our own individual life and group identity? What is needed is "deviant" seeing. A way to look inside outside, outside out and inside out and in. Perhaps deviant seeing will have an influence on how we see and come to know girls in relation to a curriculum that flickers with experience.

beth—in an already interpreted world

## IN AN ALREADY INTERPRETED WORLD

CRUCIFY every finger in the room is pointing at me I wanna spit in their faces then I get afraid of what that could bring I got a bowling ball in my stomach I got a desert in my mouth figures that my COURAGE would choose to sell out. (Amos, 1991)

"It's funny how people with disabilities only focus on their disabilities" a woman tells me at my 1995 American Educational Research Association poster session. It's funny...only focuses on disabilities. I am necessarily troubled by this response to Beth's photograph. An interpretation outside of her photograph leaves little space for possibility. Can I really walk in another person's shoes? I have come to believe I cannot, and perhaps, the most I can hope for is a space to wonder, imagine, and question. Can I ever really know or presume to know? The most I can do is listen, hear, see and hopefully understand.

This woman's words said nearly 10 months ago troubled me then just as they do now. I remember wanting to say, "No, no, no, you've got it all wrong, that is not Beth's story, you've never met Beth, never spoken to her, you have never listened, you don't know her." I felt the tightening in my body when she said, "That's all they see." Her words left me resisting the sense of what she was trying to say. I wanted to stop her from looking at Beth's photographs, push her away, ask her to leave. I did not.

Since then I have thought deeply about what is behind the reading of, in this case, Beth's photograph. I had never met this woman before, she was a stranger responding to my girls' work. I was trying to learn from a stranger. I could see no physical disability, and the woman never shared with me that she herself had a disability. And yet, I remember watching her quick gaze, her glance, clipping a moment of this particular photograph followed by an immediate response. She never asked for a story nor looked for other information; I heard a simplistic statement with high inference:

Just as I could say, "that's a heart, that's a lung. "We go through life," saying, "I must be in love," "Oh, this is seasickness," "This is an orgasm," "This is a midlife crisis." We are ready with culturally constructed labels long before we encounter the realities, even to the point of saying, "This is a heart attack," "I must be dying." We can call our fate by name before we meet. It will not retreat, but we are often relieved when doctors name our conditions. (Bateson, 1994, p. 5)

Her response agitated me. It is just not that easy. Not because she was "wrong" or that it was "untrue," but rather that she had already interpreted Beth's experience without knowing insights I had come to learn about Beth throughout our engaged relationship. What happens to girls' photographs if we respond without the story, name their experience? It is this kind of response that leaves me wondering what will be missed, dismissed, ignored, ultimately evaded from girl's experiences that have been seen in constructing their visual narratives in a world of captivity that is already interpreted.

I am not naive; I know that I cannot stop her or anyone from reading into what they read, but I have a responsibility. As a researcher, I am mindful of othering the girls' visual narratives. Therefore, I struggle in the re/presentation of how girls' images will be seen, and ultimately read, which in turn might affect their lives. What will it mean to see girls' lives visually? It is not enough for me to simply show. It is not enough for me to simply accept that I have no control over the meaning people bring to the photographs. And yet, I also know that is impossible for me to evoke an appropriate response, nor would I want to. This creates a research dilemma. I think about how the girls' visual narratives will be captured in an "already interpreted" world.

So, at the very least, how might I create a pause for others to stop, to really look and listen to the girls' experiences with photography. Is it possible to see without "already made interpretations?" Herein lies my struggle with an already interpreted world. Can we see a different way, make different connections to the photographic work created by girls? Can we see an "amputated leg" without bringing in our existing knowing/interpretations? Was this an accident? Birth defect? A dis-ease? Beth's photograph challenges images produced in fashion and media advertising as well as in the medical profession. Spence (1995) writes,

> It should be possible to talk about health and aesthetics as a duality. Women who are involved in illness should think more of documenting the processes, not as a "personal problem" (though they are) but as a way of making visible what is done to people and is never talked about openly. It might then be possible at least to discuss things more within one's family, at most to go public with them. (p. 139)

Will these photographs attract voyeuristic readers? What happens to girls when I make the personal public, knowing the personal becomes political? I continue to struggle with making the girls' camerawork public.

I was intentional in choosing to work with still photography because it slows down time, places images into units of memory that can be studied through stories that can be retold. Their images, epics, are narratives told through storied experiences over time. Together we construct and reconstruct meaning about experiences lived:

> But new plots require us to intervene for social as well as educational change. As long as we limit ourselves to educational institutions, even as we make feminist knowledge, we bind ourselves and other women to old plots. We can revise, amend, and even scrap the materials we have on hand, but only to employ our telling stories in narratives whose conventions are always already there. New plots require us to rejoin feminist inquiry and social activism. (Hartman & Messer-Davidow, 1991, p. 29)

I want "photography that listens." And yet, how can we listen to photographs in an already interpreted world? As a researcher I am attentive to what I show and tell about the images. Does this make me matriarchal? I continually ask myself if I can really expect a different response? It is a strange prejudice that sets a higher value on depth rather than on breadth and which accepts superficial as meaning "not of wide extent" but "of little depth," which for me seems decidedly on the surface (Engerer & Wuohela, 1997). I know the girls deserve space, possibility to have their photographs seen in multiple ways. Photographs simplify yet complicate the photographer's story by partializing life. Talking about a photograph slows time into units of meaning that I can study. In describing and reacting to photographs, I have experienced discomfort as I touch pockets of strong feelings of difference. This keeps me mindful to what Bateson (1994) writes about issues of difference while questioning the double helix of what when "listening to cynical remarks...particularly those in the public eye—and synthesizing these into the conviction that an entire people could be always devious and insincere. We fail to hear in the implied comparisons. Dangerous compared to what? Insincere compared with whom? Outside danger may be a part of the comfort of home" (p. 36). What can I do to disrupt the comfortable institutionalized indexical nature of photography and story?

## ANALYSIS OF CONTENT

*these are the ones?*

So these are the ones?
These are the ones you did?
Yeah, and so many negatives
they were on different film

because my mom keeps snitching my camera
and takes pictures
of my sister and my grandparents

That's a new one
a new one?
Yeah, that's what I did
You've spun that off this roll?
Two rolls
72 photographs
Yeah, that's my shots
Oh, Okay.
Actually and this is too.
Oh, wow

The girls and I created data: enormous amounts of data. I wrote in my notes about my panic in getting the girls to come back with film, that I would then have to have processed, and that we would then have a conversation with those photographs:

Ahhh, the panic of being the researcher, do I phone her and ask for the finished film. Jean suggests a letter and Merle tells me to write about it as a research issue. The realities of working with high school girls or just busy lives. Two weeks later she brought over her photographs— two rolls.

All of our one-to-one conversations about their photographs were taped and transcribed as the primary data source. As well, I used the etc's of data in the research with the girls, the scribbled washed out words from bits of paper from periodic telephone conversations, my reflections from car conversations, shared dinners, and observations from attending art productions of the girls—field notes. Pictured through cameraworks, we permitted ourselves a space and a language to construe an understanding of the evaded and how they experienced creating their own images. Photographs we mutually analyzed are from the four cameraworks: 1) projective photographs; 2) making metaphors; 3) collecting culture; and 4) family photo albums. Moving on: Each girl created between 80–140 images with Fugi and Kodak Quicksnap cameras, and two girls borrowed my Canon T50. The following images the girls created were included for our analysis:

Beth 80 photographs     Morgan 80 photographs
Maeve 127 photographs     Thya 99 photographs

## CAMERAWORKS I

### Projective photographs

projective as pertaining to
noting a technique
for revealing
evaded accounts
or underlying
structures
by the use
of ambiguous
or unstructured analysis
as ink blots—cloud pictures
cartoons
that encourage spontaneous responses

As a way to start the conversation and hear stories of what matters to girls, I invited them to the projective cameraworks by talking with them about their perceptions, values, and expectations. In the following projective photographs we attempted to deal with the ways we construct meaning from any photograph. The projective component of understanding photographic meaning underlies interactions between people and photographs. In the following conversation, Morgan speaks about her desire to project feelings, in this case, sadness, a depressed mood with a camera.

Morgan (94-12-02)
Cameraworks I
Projective photographs

See, for me, it's going to be hard because I have to decide what my goals are and my feelings are and how I want to plan it, to me that's wrong. It has to be specific. I don't want it to be spontaneous where it is just meaningless. I thought I'm feeling sad, and I'm just realizing that

*Will the girls create what they want? What do they think I want? I think about how projecting meaning onto the photographs is integral with our looking at them. What does that mean for girls?*

*This is one of my first conversations, and I think about "wrong" and the words of Arbus (1972):*
I hate the idea of composition. I don't know what a good composition

I'm in such a depressing mood. I just want to take a picture of myself, but I'm not going to get what I want. I've been experimenting with ways to try to get photographs to show my feelings, but I want the camera not to be seen. is. I mean I guess I must know something about it from doing it a lot and feeling my way into it and into what I like. Sometimes for me composition has to do with a certain brightness or a certain coming to restness and other times it has to do with funny mistakes. There's a kind of rightness and wrongness and sometimes I like rightness and sometimes I like wrongness. Composition is like that. (p. 10)

In *Photographing the self*, Ziller (1990) provides coded orientations for photographs; they are limited, but they provide a sense of framing what the girls photographed in the cameraworks:

Results: Photographic orientations

Activity
Aesthetic
Animals
Cars
Drugs
Dyad
Family
Groups
Hedonic tone
Inside
Music
People
Popular culture
Religion
School
Self
Sports

I borrowed these coded orientations as a beginning, to look and to frame the girls' projective cameraworks:

Beth
12 photographs: Aesthetic; Dyad; Hedonic tone; Music; Inside; School; Family
grandmother's gift of piano; sister; sister's tattoo; coffee shop narrative; bedroom lights; guitar; girl and son; school friends

Maeve
11 photographs: Aesthetic; Religion; Self; Inside; Outside
home shots, birthday cake, ballet photograph; trees, shadow shot, candles and Bible

Morgan
16 photographs: Aesthetic; Dyad; School; Hedonic tone; Inside; Outside
girls friends and strangers; pregnant schoolgirl; aesthetic nature

Thya
19 photographs: Drugs; Hedonic tone; Dyad; Popular culture; Food; Family; Aesthetic; Inside; Outside; Activity; Sports
boyfriend; skateboarding; food narrative; niece sleeping; birthday party; sister; ballet photograph; party narrative

Listening to the stories the girls told of selected photographs unearthed questions:

What about a title? What is the story that goes with this photograph? Ask the photograph its name, what it means and whether it has anything to tell you.
Is there anyone you know who you would like to have this photograph?
Consider the thoughts, feelings, memories, and fantasies that you have become aware of in this photograph.

## CAMERAWORKS II

### Metaphors of self: Working with self-portraits

A photograph is not only as an image, it holds a story, an interpretation of the real, a trace of life, of something that is held to be unchanging. The girls' visual narratives are surrounded by mutually constructed meaning.

Their photographs point to where they have been, as well, to a way where they might be going. Working with self-portraits evokes a memory in our lives, a memory around which we construct and reconstruct stories.

Maeve (94-11-29)
Cameraworks II
Metaphors of self

It was just sort of after I started to become happy again and this one is (laughs). I took it of myself just to get rid of the film; and it's a face that I make often, but I don't realize that I am very, very active and vivid. I guess, I'm quite a character when I talk. I use my hands and my face a lot and (laughs) we just think it's priceless to have it hanging in her locker. It's totally hilarious. It just makes everybody laugh because it totally doesn't look like me at all. Like I've never seen myself look like that at all but everybody else does. Whenever I am talking. I can't even do it now.

*What sense is made from the camera-works. Later the girls tell me they actually took photographs of things that mattered to them.*

*What do we see in ourselves?*

Looking at self-portraits, making metaphors, I framed the girl's camera-works:

Beth
31 photographs: Aesthetic; Dyad; Hedonic tone; Self; Music; Inside; School; Family; Activity; Pets; Outside
bedroom narrative; Cree-sweet grass; school locker; piano narrative; leg; prosthesis; Einstein; cat; self; mother; school friends; drama narrative; swing; outdoor nature; father's house

Maeve
35 photographs: Self; Family; Activity; Inside; Hedonic tone: Dance

ballet toes; ballet photograph; self "body" narrative; "light and dark" narrative; ballet dance narrative; sister and brothers; mother; bedroom; bathroom; self sleeping; self studying

Morgan
16 photographs: Aesthetic; Dyad; School; Self: Family; Hedonic tone; Sport; Inside; Outside
self in mirror; father narrative; drawing of self; trees; leg and candle; martial arts; mother and sister; girlfriend; coffee shop narrative

Thya
54 photographs: Drugs; Hedonic tone; Dyad; Popular culture; Dance; Food; Family; Aesthetic; Inside; Outside; Activity; Sports; Cars
Film 2(1)—trunk narrative; boyfriend; party narrative; family Christmas; boyfriend and sister narrative; niece sleeping;
Film 2(2)—car narrative; ballet dance narrative; boyfriend; dance school; self studying; "niece" babysitting

## CAMERAWORKS III

### Collecting culture

### Self-portraits taken by others

Here the girls were invited to have new photographs created of themselves by a significant other, posed and not posed images, a space to learn from seeing other perspectives, and I framed the girl's collecting culture from cameraworks III:

Beth
37 photographs: Aesthetic; Dyad; Hedonic tone; Self; Inside; School; Activity; Outside; Cars
self at school narrative; girlfriend bedroom night; school hallway narrative; school locker; teacher; car story

Maeve
9 photographs: Self; Family; Activity; Inside; Hedonic tone; Body; Aesthetic
36 photographs: Self; Cars; School; Inside; Dyad; Hedonic tone
Film 3(1)—art; music; violin; family-sister; girlfriends; self as photographer; self in bathtub; legs

Film 3(2)—fashion modeling narrative; trees; sister; body narrative; ballet pain narratives; drawing; aunt's dress; light and dark narrative; Film 3(3)—36 photographs: Self; Dyad; Hedonic tone; Body; Food; Inside; Outside; Activity; Car
body; ballet toes; girlfriend party night; school hallway narrative; school studying narrative; car narrative

Morgan
38 photographs: Aesthetic; Dyad; School; Self; Hedonic tone; Inside
self school hallway narrative; home/house narrative; architecture; school art; me and my cat; school friends; teacher; trees; bird

Thya
26 photographs: Self; Hedonic tone; Dyad; Popular culture; Food; Family; Aesthetic; Inside; Outside; Activity; Sports; Cars; Dance
self in ballet outfit; trunk narrative; ballet picture; boyfriend and party narrative; food/cooking; sisters; ballet toes; car narrative

## CAMERAWORKS IV

### Family photo albums

Why are the family photo albums where the most shadows are?

Beth
We never had this camerawork experience. I am assuming this never happened for several reasons. No time. Relationship was different. Too personal. Too close to the evaded. I can imagine Beth's photographs before cancer. Perhaps there are few photographs or no albums put together. I know that my own albums stopped being put together after Chloé's accident. The images of her feet at birth and now are painful to look at. At no time did I ever feel that Beth needed to share this camerawork with me. I am just aware and mindful to what is private.

Maeve
I looked at pictures from her babyhood, siblings and family members. This was a enjoyable and happy interview. I know Maeve's siblings since they play tirelessly with my daughter in our home. I have a deep sense of connection with Maeve through her brother and sister. This family album lets in more light for me to see Maeve's stories.

Morgan
Unfamiliar family stories, for me, cautionary stories told around the images of adults in her life. A biker's photograph was revealing and opened stories of her mother's strength and change in her life. Morgan's birth was a transformation for her mother.

Thya
Her family album included no photographs of Thya. She was not aware of this until we reached the end of the book. Thya shared painful stories of abuse, lives filled with confusion, that texture her daily life.

Cameraworks IV was a personal, very private experience, and I struggle in the representation of the family photo albums work. Much is missed. I turn to Spence (1995) for making meaning of my intention to work with the girls' family photo albums:

> Existing family album photographs [can be used] as a basis for telling stories and beginning to unmask memories with a sympathetic listener or in a workshop or collective situation. The agenda for this is always set by the context, the degree of trust and the underlying goal of the process. (p. 172)

## WRITING THE LIGHT

> We think of our eyes as wise seers, but all the eye does is gather light. Let's consider the light harvesting. As we know, the eye works a lot like a camera; or rather, we invented cameras that work like our eyes. (Ackerman, 1990, pp. 232–233)

Writing the light explores my sense making of seeing girls' photographs and hearing stories told about them; this is a mode of construction, a way of coming to understand my visual narrative method. Berger (1980) writes about difficulties in negotiating gaps between what photography and writing on photography are and should be. I see my work as fragmented across a range of sites, and by gauging contrasting positions on photography, my attempt to bind the photograph back to its ordinary context is impossible/implosion. What is seen is, at times, bewildering. I observe, study, perceive, watch, inspect, recognize, detect, identify and discern in seeing the girls' cameraworks. I distinguish and discriminate between them; I glimpse, spot, notice, spy, and catch sight of them. I see under them, over them, the difference between them, the condition they are in, if they are in trouble, what caused it, and how to listen. Placing the photograph within a web of narrative is designed to authenticate its substance, that which is depicted, in order to make the image "tell its true story."

Can visual narratives recast girlhood educational theory and research practice? How might I provide an innovative and provocative point of entry, an alternative discourse that will contrast and thicken existing traditional developmental, psychological, and educational discourses on girls? Will seeing the girls' photographs create possibilities for alternative insights? I hope their cameraworks and stories will be reread as eye-opening, disturbing, and inspiring. Like Barthes (1981), I look for what is behind the concealed as I think about how the images girls make might challenge symbols of girlhood:

It is no longer the myths which need to be unmasked, it is the sign itself which must be shaken; the problem is not to reveal the (latent) meaning of an utterance, of a trait, of a narrative, but to fissure the very representation of meaning, is not to change or purify the symbols, but to challenge the symbolic itself. (p. 69)

On the other hand, Hebdige (1988), Rosler (1989b), and Mitchell (1992) question what photographs seem to say. According to Mitchell (1992), "They do not seek to recover or retrieve the truth captured in the image but rather liberate the signifier from the constraints imposed upon it by the rationalist ideology of representation" (p. 164). He argues that digital imaging dramatically changes the rules:

Potentially, a digital "photograph" stands at any point along the spectrum from algorithmic to intentional. The traditional origin narrative by which automatically captured shade perspective images are made to seem causal things of nature rather than products of human artifice—recited in support of their various projects by Bazin, Barthes and Berger, Sontag and Scruton—no longer has the power to convince us. The referent has come unstuck. (p. 30)

And yet, to our human eye, others argue the photographs seem to bond image to referent with superglue. Can the symbol/image/signifier ever change for girls? Learning to disrupt the subject of other dichotomies troubles understanding girls' lives. Apart from the interactive process of my visual research work, I have found that the girl's photographs and stories challenge the discourse of making schoolgirl culture, and this leaves me wondering about distinctions between, for instance, good and bad, legitimate and illegitimate, style and substance, entitlement and exclusion, pleasure and danger, and the task of disrupting the authority of the impermeability of those distinctions.

Understanding my specific visual research practices and their possible meanings has meant a twofold approach. I have worked alongside approaches to art criticism and personal experience methods, as guidelines, not inflexible rules, as I trouble my re/writing of the girls' camera work. I work between the frames of traditional/conventional/modernist "principles of art elements" (Blake, 1981; English, 1988; Leland, 1990; Paley, 1995) and elements of "personal experience" research methods (Clandinin & Connelly, 1994). Together, these elements may be seriously played with for particular ends to my visual narrative inquiry. This has meant recognizing and understanding self in relation to the coconstruction of "field texts." I am mindful of privileging my "epistemological status of them" (p. 419). I have captured but a few of the stories the girls told and showed me, and Casey (1995) reminds me that "the repertoire of stories still waiting to be told (and studied) is practically limitless. What better way to grapple with making sense of our rapidly changing world than through the study of stories" (p. 240)? For this writing, I resituated myself within a postmodern aesthetic practice as an attempt to author, to map, with an intelligent and an imaginative (i/eye) as I bring together some sense of order, direction, and injunction of writerly possibility to the data chaos while resisting regularity, logic, or symmetry. A freeplay of writing the light glories in contradiction and confusion of uncomfortable practices:

Art whatever it may be is exclusively political. What is called for is the analysis of formal and cultural limits (and not one or the other) within which art exists and struggles. These limits are man and different intensities. Although the prevailing ideology and the artists try in every way to camouflage them, and although it is too early—the conditions are not met—to blow them up, the time has come to unveil them. (Haacke, 1975, p. 72)

In my visual research, the girls and I attempt to unveil the evaded. The task of placing together photographs and stories is daunting. Issues of re/representation, signature and interpretation plagued much of my work:

I cannot agree that "the world is the product of interpretation" alone; the world is also the product of human activity. Point of view—how we as concrete historical agents understand the world—must become standpoint—the position from which we try to change the world. At this time, the similarities among various feminist perspectives-radical, socialist, lesbian, heterosexual, black, white—may be more crucial than their differences. When it comes to acting in the world, even when the world is nothing more than academy, it is often to our disadvantage, indeed our survival, to act from one standpoint. (Zimmerman, 1991, p. 97)

How would acting from one standpoint look? The researcher and artist within me senses a desire to pursue separate visions, multiple ways of seeing. Who sees potential when the rest of us are blind? I have been searching for a way of coming to know, to make meaning of the interpretations expressed in my visual narrative research. Perhaps this research is like a collage of layer yet harmonized viewpoints. Johnson (1987) addresses a possibility for me to make sense of our world, a language to understand scripts of the institutional world in which we live:

Meaning includes patterns of embodied experience and preconceptual structures of our sensibility....These embodied patterns do not remain private or peculiar to the person who experiences them. Our community helps us interpret and codify many of our felt patterns. They become shared cultural modes of experience and help to determine the nature of our meaningful, coherent understanding of our "world." (p. 14)

A metaphor I think about is of a mirror my family owned when I was a girl. A fold out three-way mirror in our bathroom allowed for a multiplicity of points of view. An endless look I recognize when I look in a mirror. I think about the other mirror, the one set opposite, in front and beside that creates infinite vision, as reflections reflect one another. What mirrors are set by my hands and by those of another body? How do I act when so many mirror handlers and so many reflections are simultaneously apparent. Each mirror could be viewed separately, with complete attention to its meaning in the face of recognizing only one. But viewed together, one through/against the other, a multidimensional story surfaces: "Our perspectives—of class, race, sexuality, political persuasion—are not discrete entities...perspectivity, rather, involves the continual layering and deepening of visions in communication, not in competition, with each other" (Zimmerman, 1991, p. 97). At a glance, these are terms of coming to know my visual knowing; it is the conditions of a practice that I re/work with/against/through to create "visual narrative terms" (Bach, 1997c):

| art elements terms | personal experience inquiry terms |
|---|---|
| Unity | Situation |
| Harmony | Standpoint |
| Contrast | Intentionality |
| Rhythm | Time/rhythm |
| Repetition | Continuity/temporal |
| Gradation | Signature/Voice |
| Balance | Contemplation |
| Dominance | Interaction/Relationship |

**Visual narrative moments**

watching/peripheralvision/inventiveness
re(con)textualizing/opportunity/nuance
distortion/tilt/frame
intertextuality/relationality/tone
disrupt/deny/subvert
discord/difference/discomfort
recurrence/repetition/return
pulse/risk/implosion

Coming to terms with visual narrative practice, it is my wish to extend Ziller's (1990) content analysis in my reading of seeking out an affiliation with other practices, with nonhierarchical "moments" as a way to celebrate girls' photography and stories. My intention in placing these words together is to provide a sense of the thickness of the work, the layering over time and space. Perhaps these visual moments simply help me to fill some gaps in our understanding of looking at girls' photographs, and this is my way to compliment girl's camerawork. I consider "moment" as an "indefinite point in time with an undetermined duration or nonspecific geographical location or place" (Rosenau, 1992, p. xiii), which makes me think of a "visual narrative moment" as a possible stage/step/move of analyzing visual narrative inquiry. Mixing elements of old and new creates a sort of "pastiche...a freefloating, crazy-quilt, collage, hodgepodge patchwork of ideas or views" (p. xiii) to analyze visual narratives. Connecting elements of art design and personal experience methods, and already interpreted principles, I trouble the essentialism of these pregiven assumptions and seriously play with a "visual narrative moment" as a way to look behind the foundations and challenge "symbols, signs and fictions" of schoolgirl culture. In composing visual narrative research, we "tear back the veil" (Morrison, 1987, p. 110) and provide alternative sites of coming to know girls; an opportunity to see, again, with fresh eyes.

## EIGHT VISUAL NARRATIVE MOMENTS

In writing the stories with images from the girl's camerawork, I take responsibility of re/presenting them. I would, however, feel arrogant/pretentious/maternalistic if the narratives were read as one truth. After watching and seeing the girls and being in relation with them and my preoccupation with the missing discourse of how (the evaded) plays itself out in girls' lives, I offer my re/presentation that has been mutually constructed by girls and myself with "the veil drawn [aside]" (Morrison, 1987, p. 110). Turning to Greene (1991), my hope is that by writing around and showing the girls' photographs a space will open to go in search for the missing, of what is ignored and what is not seen:

There have to be disciplines, yes, and a growing acquaintance with the structures of knowledge, but, at once, there have to be the kinds of grounded interpretations possible only for those willing to abandon "already constituted reason," willing to feel and to imagine, to open the windows and go in search. (p. 122)

watching/peripheralvision/inventiveness

I work hard to see
to turn my eyes out
and look to the outlying/surrounding
encircling prey
while living on the margins
watching for
the evaded

I watch for prey, sneaking up behind/beside me, with open eyes. I am alert to seeing. Looking puts emotional pressure on me to learn from seeing. I use peripheral vision to inform my understanding as I picture possible compositions of making girl culture. First, my practice is located in watching by learning from seeing through/with/against other sites of representations:

Look in the mirror. The face that pins you with its double gaze reveals a chastening secret: You are looking into a predator's eyes. Most predators have eyes set right on the front of their heads, so they can use binocular vision to sight and track their prey. Our eyes have sep- arate mechanisms that gather light, pick out an important or novel image, focus it precisely, pinpoint it in space, and follow it; they work like top-flight stereoscopic binoculars. Prey, on the other hand, have eyes at the sides of their heads, because what they really need is peripheral vision, so they can tell when something is sneaking up behind them. (Ackerman, 1990, p. 299)

In my view, visual narratives make visible the invisible and can be seen as sites to make meaning while documenting and making girl culture.

the i/eye
seeing, secret secret surroundings
met with recognition
rather than bewilderment
seeing to know
from the out(lying)
stories
telling telling stories
of silence
laughter
by encircling predators
of being watched
haunting life
on the margins
resisting
what brings them
together
only peripheral visions brings them together

What makes it fiction is the nature of the imaginative act: my reliance on the image—on the remains—in addition to recollection, to yield up a kind of a truth. By "image" of course, I don't mean "symbol"; I sim- ply mean "picture" and the feelings that accompany the picture. (Morrison, 1987, p. 112)

I have photographed since girlhood. My favorite memories are in making art, in particular, photographing my world. I feel a direct connection when working with photography and narrative experience. Bateson (1994) addresses my thinking on restorying and learning:

Spiral learning moves through complexity with partial understanding, allowing for later returns. For some people, what is ambiguous and not immediately applicable is discarded, while for others, much that is unclear is vaguely retained, taken in with peripheral vision for possible later clarification, hard to correct unless it is made explicit. Beyond the denotations lie unexplored connotations and analogies. (p. 31)

But what is memory? "The act of imagination is bound up with memory" (Morrison, 1987, p. 119). This allows work to invite multiple readings, which leads me to question how we educate the imaginative act? Who is shaping the imaginative act? Whose signature marks and remarks the imaginative act?

What I am concerned with here is a process of educating the imagination. The role played by the imagination both in cognitive and moral life is often underestimated in philosophical discussion. But the fact that one cannot know everyone intimately so that one can be in a position to move empathetically beyond instances one has taken the trouble to know well to other, apparently, instances. Such responsible cognitive endeavor seems to be essential to moral life in which engagement with other people as the people that they are is a serious concern. (Code, 1991, p. 96)

## Distortion/tilt/frame

The same photograph seen in a different context is interpreted very differently. Apart from the interactive process of conversations about the photographs, we began to see the layers of multiple meaning:

Whilst we know, intellectually, that photographs are not "real," do not "tell the truth," but are specific choices, constructions, frozen moments, edited out of time, yet we invest them with meaning. Still, most people believe that photographs have the power to signify "truth." It is this contradiction and tension that is so productive. (Spence, 1995, pp. 173–176)

This contradiction and tension is a necessary part of my research process. As I view the girls' camerawork and witness their vacillating stories, it becomes apparent that "truth" is a construct and that the girls' identities are fragmented across many "truths." Selecting a standpoint, framing a story, and choosing the photograph expose moments of intentional acts:

Documentary photographer Lewis Hine remarked that, "while photographs may not lie, liars may be photographers." Many serious photographers (though not amateurs who use auto-exposure, autofocus, point and shoot cameras) also regard manipulation of exposure and focus variables as important means for realizing their intentions. (Mitchell, 1992, p. 30).

This opens questions of truth and what legitimate knowledge looks like. According to Rich (1979), "Lying is done with words, and also with silence" (p. 186):

And to speak of lies we come inevitably to the subject of truth. There is nothing simple or easy about this idea. There is no "the truth," "a truth"—truth is not one thing, or even a system. It is an increasing complexity....This is why the effort to speak honestly is so important. Lies are usually attempts to make everything simpler—for the liar— than it really is, ought to be. (pp. 187–188)

An understanding of this frees up the self from the constant search for the fixity of an "ideal self" and allows an enjoyment of self as process and becoming. Visual narratives joust reality of girls' culture. This has to do with decentering and learning to pay attention to lives on the margins:

perspective, like standpoint; outlook; viewpoint; as to frame
chassis
structural case
put together
enclose
exposure
fake the evidence against

i like the panorama
being "viewy" holding triple, strong and forceful views
but not a narrowly defined theoretical commitment
narrative and point of view
a narrative truth

Our stable, centered point of view of their arduous daily tasks. The straightforward often becomes surreal, and the camera setup and angle are the vital first steps in validating the presence of the camera and spectator panning shots through

high angle shots
camera set-up
camera angle
camera placement

The most common of all camera angles is the eye-level shot, which gives the viewer a sense of following or participating in the action and dialogue. Yet it is a convention capable of archetype. An emphasis on direct, eye-level camera angles forces the viewer to respond to the medium as a technological extension of our eye; we become dutiful observers, witnesses and characters as our senses are awakened to our lived experiences.

## Opportunity/re(con)textualizing/nuance

Visual narratives composed with photographs and stories provide opportunity for making images and making meaning. The girls created textbooks of their lives: as a site/space of possibility as it alludes to the evaded curriculum in their lives. Visual narratives are specific sites for re(con)textualizing meaning around the images and stories. The images and stories are retold over time and with relationship. They reveal complex patterns, creating a multilayered experience for the viewer through photographic messages that are transparent and mysterious: "A photograph is a secret about a secret. The more it tells you the less you know" (Arbus, 1972, p. 4 ). Despite the illusion of giving understanding, what seeing through photographs really invites is an acquisitive relation to the world that nourishes aesthetic awareness and promotes emotional attachment (Sontag, 1977, p. 111).

There are interconnections, overlaps, and evolution of the visual narratives among the girls bringing the past forward and interfacing it with the present. These visual narratives create complex, conceptual works that address contemporary issues while simultaneously deconstructing the evaded curriculum. Visual narratives encourage diversity and autonomy, flexibility and openness, a site for manipulating the medium of understanding the body through its surroundings, a visual documentation of girl culture.

Slowly change a color from warm to cool, a value from light to dark, a line from thick to thin, a shape from small to large. Each girl's stories shade and shadow both the different/similar. With time I began to see gradual change, which implies movement and suggests deep space. A sharp break in gradation interrupts movement through the photograph, creating a rhythmic accent or establishing a focal point. I can unify contrasting elements by making a gradual transition between them or enhance areas that are plain and uninteresting by introducing subtle gradations of color or value.

## Intertextuality/relationality/tone

Visual narrative means an infinite complex of interwoven interrelationships, "an endless conversation between the texts with no prospect of ever arriving at or being halted at an agreed point" (Bauman, cited in Rosenau, 1992, p. 427). Absolute intertextuality assumes that everything is related to everything else.

As I gather the images and stories to compose the visual narratives, my intention is to bridge, make a picture, between our experiences and the viewers. Rather than address a specific fragment of ourselves—the unreal world of girlhood, our dreams and longings—the experiences are layered and overlap. Though a memory may be hazy or not clearly defined, we may find the meaning of it reinterpreted through the effects of time, as we reinvent ourselves through memory, knowing an "endless conversation between the texts with no prospect of ever arriving at or being halted at an agreed point." My desire is that you, the reader, see the "infinitely complex interwoven interrelationships" (Bauman, cited in Rosenau, 1992, p. 427) in the girls' photographs and stories.

Between frames and across contexts, in gaps, overlaps, areas of suspicion and transitivity—in such spaces, circulating between individual works and transversing national positions, some intriguing relations emerge (Butler, cited in Herron & Williams, 1996, p. 387). I read the composition of these visual narratives in juxtaposition; I think about how they have been re(con)structed and how my reading writes and rewrites itself as I read and reread them.

## Disrupt/deny/subvert

Visual narrative allows for disruption as it interrupts the dominant story of girls' culture
I see the girls' camerawork as a possibility to
deny
traverse
disagree
contravene
disapprove
cross.

Perhaps, they reveal contradictions and assumptions of girls' photographs and stories. I think about what is hiding in the light and how I conceal the other. And I wonder what might be. What if?

Girls

                                    subvert
                                      destroy
                                      overthrow
                                        ruin

or run away or copy the scripted fiction of girlhood:
    i wonder
    has it always been
    the same, being a girl ?
    from the beginning
    born a girl
    with an already interpreted
    sign/symbol/story/script
    a plan ahead of time
    a predetermined
    fate already met?

**Difference/discord/discomfort**

The girls created many harmonious photographs that are pleasing to look at—harmony emphasizes similarities in relationships. Close values, colors adjacent on the color circle, and similarities of lines, shapes and sizes are melodious. To liven up a harmonious photograph, I introduced subtle variations as we spoke about or around what was missing. Seeing some of the girls' photographs may be disorienting, creating discomfort for the viewer. Perhaps I see something more in their photographs. I see them as a unique gift that helps to explain who I am and where I have come from:

Don't ask me how I felt. The photograph is the equivalent of how I felt. No words are going to help. But few people can liberate themselves verbalizing about their work; titles act as blinder. (Adams, cited in Bolton, 1989)

The visual narratives show girls' lives situated in history; they show that the girls' photographs and stories reflect that "situatedness" and that their camerawork articulates a vision of universality that coexists in a dialectical relationship to the particular. I think about the blinders and how différance is a structuring principle that suggests definition rests not on the entity itself, but in its positive and negative references to other texts. Meaning changes overtime, and ultimately, the attribution of meaning is put off, postponed, deferred, forever (Derrida, 1981, pp. 39–40).

Although seeing a photograph may create discomfort, I have learned that both discomfort and différance is calibrated by experience, almost like a measuring instrument for difference, so discomfort is informative and offers a starting point for new understanding (Bateson, 1994, p. 15).

## Recurrence/repetition/return

Repetition provides visual clues to help move the eye about the photograph. The i/eye searches for related elements that it is receptive to. Similarities in elements reinforce the viewer's recognition of symbols, strengthens the rhythm, encourages movement, and produces patterns. Repetition directs the search so that each recurrence of a color, line, shape, or value leads my i/eye to a focal point and introduces variations of repeated elements to prevent boredom:

This contradiction between difference and repetition is intrinsic to the serial mode of production itself—a mode which proceeds from, but is not identical with, the mass production of commodities. For while mass production and the social logic of homogenization which entails work to eliminate difference (standardization), serial production reinforces a limited gamut of differences into the mass-produced object. (Owens, 1994, p. 119)

Pick up the vertical rhythms of a group of trees in a fence.
Echo a cool background color in foreground shadows.
Repeat a geometric shape in different sizes or colors like the patterns of the zebra. In my view, strong narrative repeats but never the same way twice. By recurrence/repetition/return, I mean a moment to what Dewey (1938) says when he writes, "There is no intellectual growth without some reconstruction, some remaking, of impulses and desires in the form in which they first show themselves" (p. 64).

## Pulse/risk/implosion

I've won the game
For no one knows
Rumpelstiltskin is my name! (Grimm, 1959)

Reflecting on finishing meant accepting the contradiction of being finished. I never have this sense of completion. I "should see"; I "should look"; I "should read"; and I "should write"; are the shoulds that pulse in my body,

almost to an ache, a heartbeat. Therefore, I struggle to say there is a sense
that nothing can be added or taken away:

> I will attempt to have a unified look
> but I am only fooling myself
> this experience has been
> one of learning along the way

I am listening closely to girls' questions, "following girls' inquiry into relationships as it becomes more philosophical, more critical, and more psycho-
logically and politically dangerous" (Gilligan, 1991, p. 44). Arriving in a new
place and acknowledging my feelings of discomfort/surprise presses me to
go and photograph, to make a picture as I learn along the way.
Photographing offers me a site for making meaning, a pause as I "track an
image from picture to meaning to text" (Morrison, 1987, p. 117) while I
attempt to take a fresh look at the taken-for-granted. Recollections blur
between fact and fiction, reality and fantasy, and the act of imagination
allows me into the unwritten interior of life. I think about the way I catch
my eye to evoke memories, in particular, the intertextual relations between
them. When does strangeness dwindle?

I have attempted to show visual narratives that may be read as calm or
contemplative or as aggressive and abrasive, but either way consistent. My
writing is my way of watching, looking, seeing and troubling my practices of
what is seen. My own choices of revealing the photographs and stories are as
revealing about myself as they are about the girls. My hope has been to con-
tribute excitement, attract attention, and relieve monotony about girls' lives.
I have attempted to document pieces that are integrated into an embryonic
work of visual research that is intuitively felt even before I analyze how the
imagemaker has composed it.

In my view, this research work involves venture, uncertainty, chance. It
has meant looking inside out and thinking about who I am in this research
work. I took a risk, and the girls take risks. We know we risk who we are
and who others think we are. At times, my work reads like a sudden change
of scenery on a long trip, the unfamiliar, strange, made familiar by learning
to listen.

Seeing and hearing the girls' stories of the evaded around and behind the
photographs has created tension between opposing elements of curved or
straight, smooth or jagged, big or small, simple or ornate, bright or grayed,
warm or cool. Opposites push and pull, energizing the photograph's surface
and exciting the viewer's i/eye. Risk introduces contrast to make a creative
and stimulating visual narrative. I usually think of using strong value contrast

for immediate visual impact. I also vitalize a low intensity color scheme with a sudden burst of pure color or energize flat shapes with a bold, aggressive line, a sort of implosion. Baudrillard (cited in Rosenau, 1992) writes, "The tendency for phenomena in a post-modern world [is] to explode inwardly, thus destroying themselves and one's assumptions about them. Meaning disappears altogether" (p. 57).

I see the girls' visual narratives explode inwardly and subvert traditional scripts:

When it's raining but the sun is shining, or at a misty waterfall, sunlight hits the prism like drops of water and split into what we call a "rainbow". On such a day, rainbows are always about, hidden somewhere behind the skirts of the rain; but to see one best, you have to be positioned just right, with the sun behind you and low in the sky. (Ackerman, 1990, pp. 244–45)

Perhaps visual narratives are a site of a societal entity that acquires significance in the presence of the viewer. The visual narrative operates under the basic premise that the photograph and the story and its viewers in any given dialogue are mutually constructing: the visual narrative and the readers share an equal responsibility in determining meaning from within any dialogical context. I wonder if a dialogue is nothing more than a monologue. Visual narratives make no truth claims. Co/constructed narratives, fragmented across a range of sites, are stories I have written, an attempt to show the teller's point of view based on her experience with the camerawork. I parallel my stories of coming to know girls and myself differently through/against/with

> every impulse of light exploding
> from the core
> as life flies out at us. (Rich, 1979, p. 47)

The visual narrative is achieved through a dialogue between: a) my presentation of the human body as a personal art form; b) the historical significance of the human figure as a coded genre and its influence on contemporary constructs of the body; and c) the experiences of the viewers and their personal constructs of the body as it pertains to culture and society. By presenting visual narrative as a verb, in this manner, photography and story remain active as an agent in forming, reforming and questioning diverse aspects of making girl culture. By determining my visual narratives as presently active, I see them maintaining their historical significance, and they participate in constructing contemporary ideologies and imaginings that travel freely through space and time; they alter and form new cultural perspectives of girls. My hope is that readers will participate in a process to determine whether or not my visual narratives are painful, isolated, sexual, beautiful, disturbing, exploitive, emotionally strong or victims of circumstance.

## Contests of meaning: On the other hand

these visual narratives celebrate
the girls' camerawork
and the stories
around their photographs
knowing that
[i/eye] have been in
relation with the girls for three years
and that their visual narratives
have been
re(con)structed
[with informed consent] [with epistemic responsibility]
in relation with the girls
[i/eye] see these visual narratives
as one possibility of
brightness
there are many other stories
many other photographs
[i/eye] do not know
and do not tell
these visual narratives
offer a site
a contest for meaning making

Nothing is ever the same as they said it was. It's what I've never seen before that I recognize. (Arbus, 1972, p. 1)

Ambiguity is the warp of life, not something to be eliminated. Learning to savor the vertigo of doing without answers or making shift and making do with fragmentary ones opens up the pleasures of recognizing and playing with pattern, finding coherence within complexity, sharing within multiplicity. (Bateson, 1994, p. 9)

Over the 3 years, I have "come to know" the girls in different ways. I have learned from seeing their photographs and from hearing them tell telling stories. Through my experience, I have troubled my re/representation of the girls' camerawork as I struggle with the meaning making from this research: who interprets schoolgirl culture? who is making the knowledge claims? And if the world is the product of interpretation, then who or what determines which interpretative system will prevail?

I look at the context from which the girls' photographs were produced and the telling stories that emerged through the photographs. In my visual narrative research, "image matters," and these are "photographs that listen," and this keeps me mindful to my eyes and hands, which edit, approve and reject photographs and telling stories. I can say that each time I study a photograph I attempt to unravel layers of meaning within my personal frames of knowing to make different meanings from the photographs. The girls and I know that a camera does not just record, it also mediates. Trying to read a photograph as a book presents similar problems of believing that there is one interpretation, one truth. There is no one way to read a photograph; there is no one way to tell a story. The visual narrative troubles the activity of reference.

I see photographs having two quite distinct uses: one belonging to the private experience and one to the public experience. The meaning and stories of photographs are personal. At times, visual narratives can portray a story not intended. Each viewer's response is based on individual perceptions, filtered by frameworks of interpretation. The meaning of the photograph exists as an alliance of possibilities that occur in the connection between that person and the image itself (Rosler, 1989a; Spence, 1986; Weiser, 1993). Within our research relationship we studied: ethics of photography; the politics of looking; risks with "making public the private." In showing the following compositions, I hope to "celebrate" each girl's visual narratives, certainly not violate the trust of a friend.

On one hand:
In conversation with Beth, we talk about her love of piano, poetry and film. She has lived with cancer since she was 11. These are the first photographs she has taken of her leg, a missing body part. I think about my life, and I ask myself if I could survive what Beth has experienced. I learn of a drama teacher who dismisses Beth's reality of a phantom pain during a dress rehearsal; she was told that she was looking for attention. Could someone join in that concern and try to bridge the realities of phantom pain as a truth for amputees?

On the other hand:
Beth writes poetry from deep inside. Could someone join her there?

On one hand:
In a conversation with Maeve, I see her photographs of light and dark, and I write about not being able to see her. She shows and tells stories of her body overshadowed by a collection of images of: "damaged knees"; "bleeding toes"; "small breasts"; and "a fat butt." These are complex stories of the body in competition with the cultural expectations of being a ballet dancer. We talk about what happens when we ignore our body. Could someone join in that concern and try to understand the reflexive bodily practices in relation to ballet?

On the other hand:
Maeve talks about the crossroads of becoming a desirable woman. Could someone join her?

On one hand:
Morgan is moving. Her family is in transition, and another move means leaving her home. I am reminded of home and how we are tied to our biographies. I hear stories of desiring a relationship with her father. He lives in the same city. He does not respond to her letters. Could someone join her there?

On the other hand:
Morgan reads philosophy, books different from the ones I read. She photographs trees, branches, buildings and homes. She talks about connections to the earth and Indian life. Could someone join her there?

On one hand:
Thya wants to know if she will marry her highschool boyfriend? He is a "decent guy" according to Thya: "he talks"; "he cuddles"; "he's cute." She wants to talk about the Canadian dream of marriage. She also wants a university degree. Thya questions the "cult of domesticity" as we talk around the labor contradictions of marriage, school and romantic love.

On the other hand:
Thya acknowledges stories of abuse; hidden in the trunk are stories about the "wolf" who lives in her house. Could someone join her there?

On one hand:
I watch "herstory" pass by. I see my story: "There are always two things that happen. One is recognition and the other is that it's totally peculiar. But there's some sense in which I always identify with them" (Arbus, 1972, p. 1). As a mother, I want to tell them to have fun, play, be careful, things will be different in the morning, hoping for the fairy tale ending. I want to hug them. I do not want to judge them. I want to prevent any possible harm, nasty response, and exploitive labeling/stereotyping. I desire for them what I desire for my daughter.

On the other hand:

As a researcher, I want the girls to see multiple "truths"; scripts of possibility, different ways of "knowing"; and to experience a way out by photographing their lives. I want to challenge existing knowledge claims made about/for/on girls; I want girls to resist already interpreted experiences. I want their image/gaze to matter. I want their stories to matter. I hope "others" will join in seeing possibility, diversity, and to imagine other ways of coming to know girls.

In trying to understand, appreciate, and perhaps see the girls' worlds, I have written the following stories with the girls' cameraworks. The following stories emerge from my practice of looking. These are but a few stories from a collection of many. The stories have been reconstructed with a split text in order to portray a sense of what matters for the girls and myself. The left column re/presents our research conversations. The right column re/presents my reflections on the conversations and how they intertwine with the words of others. It is through visual narrative that I am able to approach evaded experiences with divergent views in order to consider the possibilities inherent within researching girls' lived experiences. I see the girls' stories emerging from the variations of eight narrative visual moments lived out through writing my research text. The resulting juxtapositions can and should be read in many different ways.

beth

beth

beth

# IN MY ROOM

Beth (94-11-18)
Cameraworks I
Projective photographs

*Beth's room is eclectic, artistic, and she photographed her bedroom through a panoramic view of 5 photographs, a photo-narrative. I thought about the fragility of revealing one's private life. But then I thought about what I learned from seeing Beth's bedroom.*

*I've telephoned Beth to set a time to meet, and she told me she was in her room. Now I see a part of her bedroom. The time I called she had friends in. I thought about being in her room. There's so much to read: symbols, artifacts, and words. A room full of collections of lights, advertisements, books, tins, and clothes. A room I see as full, colorful and joyous.*

Anyway, this is my room. Oh, you can even see all these little things, little squares, they're lights. It's kind of a neat picture isn't it? There's my window, window in my room, and I have, you can kind of see them, the Absolut ads. You can see there are a bunch of pages

Oh, yeah

*This photo-narrative has opened conversations.*

Those are all Absolut Vodka ads. People are thinking I'm like an alcoholic, but I just collect these ads because they're really creative. Have you ever seen Absolut Vodka ads, you know, ads, you know, of Absolut?

*This is my first taped interview with Beth, and I am not asking her if she drinks. I would not ask a friend the first time we met, "do you drink?" I think about my place as researcher and ethical ways I live out my relationships with the girls.*

Yes, but I haven't stared at them long enough to notice.

*At least not in the way Beth was saying. Now I see Absolut ads in many places, and I must say they are striking and can be read in multiple ways.*

(Laughs) I really like them, I have like Absolut Miami and Absolut L.A. and Absolut Warhol and Absolut...all these different ones, and I have over 50, which covers most of this wall, and it goes on up over here.

*Beth has a warm inviting laugh; it breaks my tension. I am nervous with Beth. I'm nervous, nervous with this uncertainty.*

Oh, neat.

*I've seen Absolut ads in a new way. In a bookstore in Chicago I saw an historical photographic book on Absolut. Made me think about the corporate story, the place of alcohol in people's lives.*

And it's interesting that you can just kind of see them and my angel picture.

*I didn't notice the angel poster. I noticed the ribbon and feathers, the Tori Amos posters. I read the words on another poster of a forest that was clear cut:*
O pardon me thou bleeding piece of earth that I am meek and gentle with these butchers.
*Next to this poster is Beth's leg brace with a bouquet of flowers in it.*

So what, they're from a magazine? I just find like magazines. I'll be at like the doctor's office or another waiting space and I'll just start ripping it out or something and then all over my room I hang stuff which I love. I love hanging stuff.

*I think about what Beth sees.*

(Further into our conversation Beth tells me again about her bedroom.)

Oh, sure, it shows so much of what Toni Morrison says, I just loved this woman's writing, she is a black writer. And she writes about the interior, the interior life, and to me these pictures show a part of your interior life, you know, literally. For real what ever that means. I mean where else would I ever get to see your room. Unless you invited me I mean. What's the likelihood of you inviting an adult, a researcher, into your bedroom.

**My room, I love my room.**

Yeah, I always have, too. I really connect with you on that. I loved my bedroom and even now, you know. It's simple, clean with straight lines, now because I like the empty space.

*I never went into Beth's bedroom, not for real, but after looking at her bedroom photographs I think differently about the private made public.*

*Salinger (1995) writes about remembering her friends' bedrooms. She has composed a photographic book about teenagers' bedrooms. She tells a story about going into homes of strangers and going into bedrooms. My bedroom was a private place. Like Salinger, as an adolescent, I became "aware of the power to define and revise one's image through decor" (p. 2).*
*I was not allowed to have boys in my room. My walls were covered with images from 70s popular culture; pictures from movies and advertising layered the wood paneling. Framed photo collages marked important times of my lived experiences. My best friend had pink walls and white French Provincial furniture. Eventually, her walls turned to mauve, and she got*

*new shag carpet. My cousin had paint-ed black walls with dark purple cur-tains. His bedroom story raised eye-brows and brought out questions. My highschool boyfriend's bedroom walls were painted a skyblue, a darker toned bedspread covered the double bed that was pushed against the wall. A clean homogeneous look, a stiff-shirt look. There was a mirrored dresser trimmed with photographs and a glass jar of pennies. I remember thinking he'd be cooler.*

I figure once I get my own place, my room would probably be more, but I'm collecting like all this stuff and its like, have you ever seen *Labyrinth.*

No.

*I think of when girls move away from home. I remember moving to Vancouver at 18. Starting to build a home, alone and then with my boyfriend.*

Well there's this one character and she collects things, everything she finds like she lives in a junkyard, and she got such a big pack on her back. So she has this huge mound of stuff on her back, its huge, I mean she's a puppet.

This sounds like something's good.

Have you ever heard of it?

No,

It's so Labyrinth. She carries every-thing with her. It's kind of just in case. And in my room I have everything. I bought a teapot. I saw this teapot and I bought and it is really crazy. So I always talk about, I have, if I had a house, my house I'd always have my stuff spread all over my house.

*An enigma.*

*A puzzling problem. Hearing and relistening to Beth's words I still miss what is said.*

I can see you.

*I loved living in Vancouver, and I can imagine Beth living in an unfamiliar place while she learns along the way.*

Exactly.

In my apartment in Vancouver I had all these posters.

So I have a whole house in my room, it's my life, it's my house, like I mean it's my house, and my mom has, like pictures she has in the living room. I'm like, mom, take it down, but of course she likes it.

*I think about "house," "home," and rooms we live in and learning as coming home. I think of decor and of how I arrange and rearrange the spaces in which I live.*

next photograph

beth

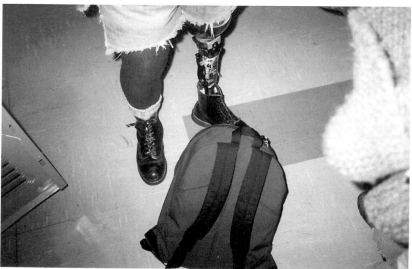

beth

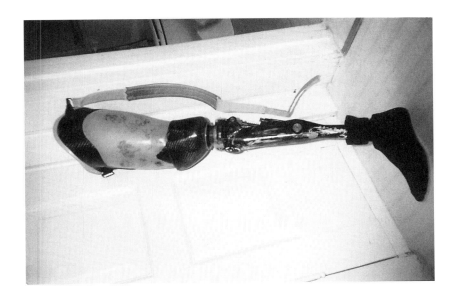

beth

## PIANO

Beth (94-11-18)
Cameraworks 1
Projective photographs

That's my piano. See this is, I don't know why I take pictures. I really forget why I take pictures of these things. There's something about the plants and everything.

*I have little doubt that talking about the photographs is a different experience for girls. This is our first conversation. Having time to talk with Beth is cool. Do the girls take photographs around the cameraworks I set up at the end of our conversations? What is Beth projecting in her photographs of her piano.*

Well, it's like the whole music thing because music is like my life, and for Maeve, you know, she loves to dance and all my friends, you know for some people it's dance and for Morgan and Jackie, it's the visual arts. They both draw a lot and express themselves that way, and I just love to play the piano. It's my best friend. Oh, it's so beautiful. (Laughs) So, that's my piano, and it's so special.

*I know. She names two girls in the study, and I think about how the girls connect their learning to the subcultures of the arts. Later, I learn Jackie would have liked to be in this study. I feel haunted by the question of who is in? who is out?*

*Oh, so beautiful. What is beautiful?*
*I think a lot about where girls make sense of their life desires and loves. What's decided for girls in an already interpreted world?*
*I think about people who own things. Having an instrument for self, having the privilege of playing.*

And it is yours?

Yes, my grandmother gave it to me when I was 8 years old and that's when I started playing.

*I remember my friend's piano, playing with her, the pleasure of making music together. We laughed and cried on the piano stool. I remember her playing. Her mother made her play. I was a hack. Her piano stood against the family room wall. Photographs lined the top of it, images and stories marked histories of generations of Janet's family. But those photographs are only pieces of her life. Janet, and my other friends Randy and Rob, died in a head-on collision on a long ago May weekend. I was 18. I continue to be in relation with Janet's mother. It's different now, but her piano stands in the same place.*

Oh, wow. On your own?

*How do girls learn along the way?*

Well, I took lessons for 2 or 3 years and then my piano teacher moved away and I've just stopped and I just kind of play my own now. I can't read music that well, but I play by ear pretty well.

Wow.

*I wish I made time to play my instruments. I think of the years my parents provided me with guitar and flute lessons. Who do we learn from?*

I think I'm going to start lessons again though. That's my piano, which I love. I don't know why I took a picture of it; well, that's my piano.

*I think she took a piano picture because she loves piano.*

Yeah.

*I really don't know what to say. I follow Beth's story.*

And then, there's Tori Amos, who to me is like God, I always talk about Tori Amos like she's the perfect role model. Have you ever heard of her?

*Tori Amos...*

*Beth knows a lot about her.*
*And now I listen to Tori Amos's CDs frequently.*
*God, I need a chapter on religion.*
*Perfect role model....Who matters for Beth? Who are "role models" for girls?*
*I think about writing music and reading other texts.*

Okay.

She's a singer and a pianist. She's amazing on the piano. She's just so awesome. She can just fly. I don't know how she does it. She's really amazing, and she writes all her own sheet music.

*I think about writing music and reading other texts.*

Okay.

And I just totally admire her, she's really amazing. Not that she's just talented, but she really confident, and she's like this total feminist woman, but to like the point where, I don't know, people who are like really, really feminist, they start to annoy me if they're really gung ho, and like women, women are better and to gets to more of an extreme which is pushing it the other way kind of.

*Really, really feminist...*

*I had not seen Tori perform until after meeting Beth.*
*Total feminist woman*
*Need/desire to position my feminism*
*Social feminist theory*
*Poststructural feminist*
*Postmodern feminist*

*Affirmative postmodern feminist*
*Psychoanalytic post structural "ists,"*
*"posts"*
*lists*
*names and more lists*
*isms and more ism…and artificial*
*divisions*

*Really, really feminist*
*Really gung ho*
*Solomon (1996) wrote about Amos's*
*relation with feminism in a recent*
*Shift article:*
"You've certainly become a symbol for many feminists, many victims of abuse." Amos responds, "I think the feminist movement is dead. But where it's going now, it's about human beings claiming the yin—to get very Eastern for 5 seconds.…Some feminists hate my guts, because I'm really about talking about the vulnerability now. The women that want to stay angry—and I know the angry woman, I've been there, believe—that isn't where the real power is. The feminist movement broke into a hierarchy and somehow became more controlling than that which has controlled it. It should be about no hierarchy, but how do you do that? That means no control, that means no domination. That's very tricky"(p. 38).

Yeah.

*i/eye resist positioning my self*
*for too long.…*
*Whose master narrative dominates…*
*Caricatures of feminism*
*What images do the girls have? It seems*
*to me an uneasy divide between "us"*

*and "them," a division painfully concretized by the girls stories:*
The divisions which characterized the early years of the Woman's Movement have become even more complex today, multiplying with the energy and persistence of fruit flies despite our increased awareness of them. It's not simply a gap in understanding between women and men, but between rich and poor, white and non white, straight and gay, butch and femme, Freudian and Lacanian, liberal or radical, nature and culture, parent and child, parent and childless. (Zimmerman, 1991, p. 89)

| | |
|---|---|
| But she is just really honest and confident. | *but feminism(s) matter to me…so does* *Honesty* *Confidence* *Sincerity* |
| Is she Canadian? | *Why ask this I wonder at my first read of the transcript.* |
| No. She's American, but I just love her. I just think she's so, she's inspired me. She's really strong. | *That she's really strong matters…* |
| I think one of the other girls at school mentioned her. | |
| Amos. Yeah, a lot of people, because she's kind of an alternative band woman. Well, she's not a band, but kind of an alternative singer. | |
| Oh, okay. | *Other graduate students know of…but have they listened?* |

So that people in that scene sort of know her. She's really neat. I like her a lot.

And she has a very unique voice.

Her voice, I don't know if it's really unique, it's just her music is just really unique.

Okay.

*In a interview with Amos, Solomon (1996) questions her about the affects of criticism. I reflected on what I read:* "And therefore, criticism doesn't affect you?" Amos responded, "When somebody's writing about my work, they're really writing about themselves. I believe that. Because if you want to sit down and analyze my technique, you have to acknowledge the craftsmanship. When you can't acknowledge that, I write you off. Come on, I was writing music when most kids were peeing on themselves in their bed. I mean I was playing Mozart. It doesn't mean that you like what I do, but there is a level of craftmanship." (p. 37)

She's a good singer. I wouldn't say she's like an amazing singer.

No, no.

*I think about what girls like to do…*

She's more than amazing.

Pianist.

And a really good pianist, she writes all her own music and plays the piano, and when she plays it, you should see what it's like. I'll describe it. She sits sideways on the bench because she started playing in bars when she was like 12 and people never look at her, so it's like, she

*Again I'm thinking about what I read in the Shift magazine:*
So when people say, "Tori Amos is so annoying, with her high voice and affected way she straddles the piano bench," how do you respond? "Fine. And how about she can play! What about that? That's fair. Then if you say she annoys the fuck out of me, that's fair too. You know, people are saying this is my best work and my

kind of straddles it with her right leg over the one side and then uses her left foot on the pedal, which is strange, you know, you should use your right foot and then she puts her hands like this and she always jumps up when she's playing and, she really, she like dances on the piano and she never watches her fingers, which blows my mind because I always have to watch where I'm sticking my fingers and she just totally sings and jumps up and just gets into her music and her hair that flips like, oh, she's really cool.

most challenging work and others are saying it absolutely sucks, you should burn it and urinate all over it. What's hard is when I've met someone and I'm totally misrepresented." (Solomon, 1996, p. 37)

*How are girls re/presented? Can we ever re/present ourselves?*

Oh, and where have you seen her?

I have seen her on TV and video. I have never seen her live, but I remember when I first heard her, it was on Dini Petty.

Oh really.

*I've seen the video of Little Earthquakes when I had bronchitis, i/eye ignored my body, and Beth brought over some audio tapes of Tori Amos, her biography and videos. I watched and read them. Like Beth I thought of Tori Amos as an amazing active young woman. Her experiences led me to reflect on church influences on my life. Although I am not the daughter of a preacher, Judeo–Christian values were upheld in my girlhood. Something in Amos's music captures a concealed part of myself. I like her music.*

I was like sick one day and they had her on Dini Petty. She's done concerts and stuff in Toronto and Montreal, but she's never come to Edmonton, which is a pity but that's okay.

We should try and get her here.

Yeah. But I'm going to like write to them or something. I love her. I could go on forever about her.

Oh, neat. I'll look for some of her music.

She is really cool.

I love looking at, or listening to, alternative music.

I just think she's wonderful. She's really good. A lot of articles that I've read say that she sounds very much like Kate Bush. But I've never heard Kate Bush, so I don't know, other people have said that.

*A connection, I like Kate Bush, I listen to her music...*"running up that hill to make a deal with God...."
In her recent interview from Shift, Amos was asked:
"Let's get bitchy for a second. What do you feel like when people call you a Kate Bush copycat?" She replied, "I think that it's just a reflection of them, isn't it?" (Solomon, 1996, p. 37).

Okay.

*Isn't it?*
*Copy cat?*
*What is unique?*
*Why must I compare? Or is it only to make a connection?*
*I think so.*

I guess maybe it's her voice or something.

Yeah, she's got a really unique voice.

She's kind of like Sarah McLachlan, Ani DeFranco.

*I listen carefully to music. I listen to all the music the girls mention that they listen to.*

Yeah.

That kind of scene, you know?

Yeah, yeah.

They are also very good singers. I
admire that.

I like them, too.                    *Music brings me pleasure.*

end conversation

## RETELLING BETH'S STORIES

Never was a cornflake girl thought that was a good solution hangin
with the raisins girls she gone to other side givn us a yo heave ho
things are getting kind of gross and I go sleepy time this is not really
happening you bet your life it is. (Amos, 1994)

In over a year of coming to know Beth, I had little sense of her place
within the formal school subjects, the basics, the required academics, nor did
I press or explore them, except, perhaps, in passing, a kind of educational
researcher's politeness. Mutual experiences of making music, of being productive in the subcultures of the arts, and relations with family were talked
about. I write of Beth as telling strong stories, ones about her grandmother
who had given her the gift of a piano. Beth spoke of her love of piano.
Viewing Beth's photographs invites me into a space that I had not expected.
Within her panoramic bedroom narrative, I was struck by the energy, by the
details, of her private space.

One of Beth's connections with popular culture revolves around the life
of Tori Amos—stories about her music, about her girlhood, about watching
Tori's music videos and about reading her words. This has built a connection
between Beth and myself. Hearing Beth's pull to Tori Amos means I listen,
too. I think of how Beth's words connect with the words of Tori Amos's song
*Silent all these years*, where she questions "what's so amazing about really deep
thoughts" (Amos, 1991). I see Beth having deep thoughts, knowing she will
never be a cornflake girl. Beth's school stories reveal experiences with the
evaded curriculum, the embodied experiences of living in schools, stories
rarely spoken, rarely photographed.

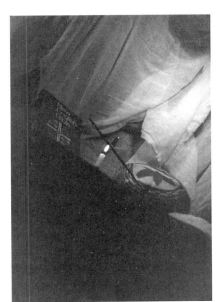

maeve

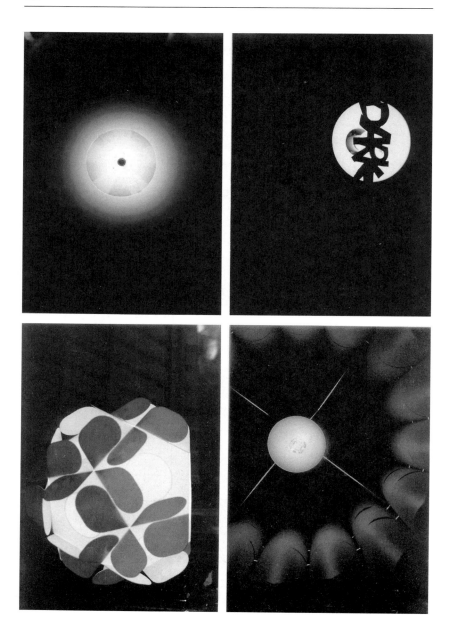

maeve

maeve

# I CAN'T SEE YOU IN THIS LIGHT

Maeve (94-11-06)
Cameraworks I
Projective photographs

*Space can be grasped in several dimensions. Maeve's first cameraworks are images of her private and public spaces of her bedroom, backyard, and places she visits.*

This is our garden. The remnants of our garden after it was all pulled up. And before we raked up all the weeds and everything, just all of the stalks and everything just sitting here in the dark. Whenever I'm home, which is not home very often in the daylight, I get kind of a pining for it because I was home for 3 years in junior high. I was really a part of the family thing, and you know, I was there to do the garden. I was there to help carve the pumpkins. I was there etc. etc.

*sitting here in the dark*

*daylight*
*Maeve was home schooled in Rudolf Steiner Waldorf philosophies until she was in Grade 8. I write of Maeve as a resister to the shortcomings of public education.*
*What becomes visible?*

(In our second conversation, Maeve talks further about light and dark.)

Maeve (94-11-29)
Cameraworks II
Making metaphor

This is just my light. I got my fingerprints all over it.

Yeah.

A first step is to allow for point light sources. Such sources distribute light evenly in all directions from a single point, but the intensity falls off with the square of the distance from the source to the reflecting surface. A flash photograph clearly shows the effect of illumination by a single point light source. Intensities of similarly colored surfaces diminish as the square of the distance that the light travels from the flash and back again to the camera: nearby surfaces are very bright, but distant surfaces fade into darkness. (Mitchell, 1992, p. 148)

And this is my

Light.

*What fades into darkness?*
*What hides in the light?*

Light in my room, and I used no flash, and I thought would look kind of neat, and it looks really neat.

Yeah, it is.

I guess what I found.

*So what's in the shadows? Is Maeve hiding in the light?*

This way? Or this way?

Oh, I have no idea. I don't remember.

Okay.

I think it was this way.

*I am thinking about how the transcripts are difficult to match up with the photographs....I see the importance of talking about the pictures.*

Or this way or something, but I got it pretty well centered.

Yeah.

This one in the flame? One that I took like the other one. Looks pretty much the same.

In reality, different types of sources not only have different shapes, but also emit light energy in characteristically different luminous intensity and spectral distributions: a candle does not produce the same spatial and spectral distribution as a halogen lamp. Comprehensive light-source models used in production of

Well, there's something about light, obviously.

You can see that it's all taped because I've dropped things so many times and it's so tacky. It's like this old plastic piece of junk and it's green and white but I love it. Like I swear, I wouldn't let them sell the house with it. It came with the house sort of thing, but I will take it with me.

Oh, we've taken ours. The one that's in our bedroom is like that.

I just like it.

It always makes me feel at home.

About the flash is that even though it brightened the room you get such a different feeling, and it's so orange and almost white around.

Yeah.

And then it's just black but not really black, kind of a reddish-black.

Oh, it's neat. Yeah, oh, okay.

sophisticated renderings must provide for the descriptions of these differences. (Mitchell, 1992, p. 150)

*I'm thinking of antique lights that we have moved with us through three homes.*
*I think of Arbus (1972): "One thing struck me very early is that you don't put into a photograph what's going to come out. Or, vice versa, what comes out is not what you put in" (p. 15).*

*I think of Maeve's knowledge of values and her ability to compare lightness and darkness, as though her eye were a camera loaded with black and white film. I also think of color vision and what that means as we observe our worlds.*

I love, I love lights. Whatever.

Yeah. Well, this. I hate to say, I do, too. But there's something there. I don't know what it is.

I don't know. I'll have to see what else comes through my pictures. It's like, wow, never the same thing.

I know.

end conversation

(In our third conversation, Maeve explores further her interest of light and dark.)

I urge each one of us to reach down into that deep place of knowledge inside herself and touch that terror and loathing of any difference that lives there. (Lorde, 1984, p. 109)

*I think about Maeve as she looks at what I see?*

Maeve (95-01-29)
Cameraworks III
Collecting culture

This one is dark.

I like that.

Another one, more playing with the lights, I just view when it's night and I turned on the lights and just fold a piece of dark construction paper and pasted it on the edges. Taking pictures it's off center, but I kind of like it like that. Do you like that?

*liking and not liking—I know it's more than that.*

Oh, the edge on the left side of the picture, I mean really artistically speaking naturally. I mean, there's that first black, there's another light, look at them all. Did you ever feel I wonder why I take these pictures?

*I wondered…*

*Maeve photographs light and dark, and it is this repeated theme that press-es me to look. Through her aesthetic photographs I am led to wonder about research relationships. Can I ever know the girls? The adventure has been to see girls—but I can't see you in this light. Caught between strong shadow and bright sunlight, I see her photographs capturing the tensions inherent in the notion of a female identity:*

*see*
>*observe*
>>*understand*
>>>*experience*
>>>>*receive*

*accompany*
*consider*

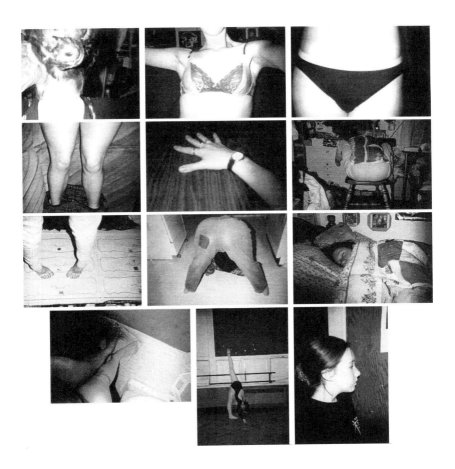

maeve

maeve

maeve

# BELLS ON MY TOES

Maeve (94-11-29)
Cameraworks II
Making metaphor

This is, I mean, this is a part of my body that I'm most comfortable with. I'm comfortable with the fact that I have no chest, and I'm okay with it. It doesn't bother me at all. Never has. I don't think it ever will because breasts get in the way in dancing, you know, and I just, I think the whole bone system, collar bones and this little, just the end of it that sticks out, I think it's really beautiful. I don't think it's beautiful in anorexia but

Given that the breast is continually and banally represented in the media, and emphasized as our most important asset, it is not strange that we would find a journey to try to include the rest of our bodies hard. (Spence, 1995, p. 139)

*you know... i /eye know*
*How do girls learn to be comfortable with parts of the body? I think about what I am comfortable with. I remember the time I've spent crucifying my body. As I un/learn to make sense of my mind body connection.*
To understand, we have to "use our heads," meaning our minds. Most people think of the mind as being located in the head, but the latest findings in physiology suggest that the mind doesn't really dwell in the brain but travels the whole body on caravans of hormone and enzyme, busily making sense of the compound wonders we catalogue as touch, taste, smell, hearing, vision (Ackerman, 1990, xix).

No.

It's beautiful when you can see them. I think they're absolutely gorgeous. So, I'm okay with that.

*Beautiful*
*Our Western notions of beauty*
*Aesthetic*

Yeah.

With sort of my shoulder area.

Oh, really, I thought, I was going "oh, wow!"

*I sense a powerful approach for Maeve's construction of her body photo-narrative, which is concerned with the flesh; the subject seems to call for close-ups, scars, marks, lumps, bumps, creases and hairs:*

[The] word made flesh: "youth culture" as sign-system centres on the body—on appearance, posture, dress. If teenagers possess little else, they at least own their own bodies. If power can be exercised nowhere else, it can at least be exercised here. (Hebdige, 1988, p. 31)

That's my face.

146

But not when I looked at the whole series, a mini-narrative. Okay.

These are just my bashed toes.

Oh.

Boo hoo, my toes. (Laughs)

It's like when I saw these, I remembered you telling me this story, so when I saw this I wasn't surprised. I thought, this so connects to your story but you know when you look at those toes.

They were pretty "ouchy" that day. That was just, it's just after I got new shoes.

Yeah.

*It was unexpected, a closeness that prompted me to write about ballet denying practices. I have struggled with making the private public and settled my discomfort by reducing Maeve's body photographs, believing that too close a focus on the purely physical body risks leaving the person behind. Maeve's cameraworks remind me that the purely physical dimension of flesh is but one thread in the body's fabric.*
*I am thinking about the pain in relation to beauty. I think about the memory work from Haug (1987) and the rites of passage, in this case, dancing rites of passage in relation to the body, of hair, legs, breasts, feet....*
*What bodily pain is felt by ballet dancers? Are ballet practices changing to the body?*
*What can they exercise with their own bodies?*
*Sore toes is a story told by both Maeve and by Thya.*

*Are they choosing stories of pain? Are they alive when they are bleeding?*

The shoes I wear are actually plastic. And plastic and glues warm to your feet better, and when you first soften these ones, they just bite.

*"they just bite"*

So, what would this photo say if it could talk?

*I am borrowing a Judy Weiser question. I have found that some of her questions throw the conversation. I find myself thinking about Weiser's therapy work, and I wonder what this kind of question leads Maeve to respond? How does it change the conversation?*

Probably, it's such a little material thing, but it totally affects you because you can't wear shoes. You're like ooo! awe! and you're like staggering around school and you feel really dumb because your toes hurt so much and you don't really know. I don't know, you don't want to show off. I hate it when people are always like "my toes are too sore. I have blisters. I'm a dancer. Ha! Ha!" You know. But, I don't know, it's like par for the course with dancing.

*I think about bodily injury and living a script of physical pain. What is the recurring damage to the body for/from dance?*
*I think about the stories girls tell in relation to the subcultures in which they live. I am not a dancer, so I am curious about the stories and the politics of the body as girls dance throughout their girlhoods. Maeve told me she started when she was 13, which, as she acknowledged, was a late age for ballet.*

Yeah.

And it's part of me. My dead toes. They're getting worse all the time like, they were, I guess, I don't know, by the time I'm 40, they're going to be pretty ugly, if I keep on dancing because they callous and every time they blister, they callous a bit more, so it's like the beginning of the end.

*What happens to women's bodies after years of physical injury? I have a friend who had been a gymnast and horseback rider who has had her spine fused from damage. She will never ride again.*

Really, so girls, dancers go around and talk about their toes. Will dancers acknowledge this pain amongst one another or to others?

*layering and building up*

Oh, God! Yeah. We're always complaining about our toes.

Okay.

*complaining*
*or telling a telling story*
*of not being heard*
*What matters?*

And you have to take really good care of them because your toenails can get ingrown so easily or anything like you have to cut your toenails specific ways and all that.

And who teaches you about that?

*Who do we learn from?*

You learn by trial and error, and some teachers will give you advice if you ask, but lots of times their ideas don't work for you.

Oh, okay. So, this practice is a rite of passage sort of thing?

I would say so. I mean now it's a pain in the ass to have blisters and whatever. I'm like "oh man" but at first it was so like "yes, we have blisters, we have pointe shoes, yes, yes." It was such a big deal to have my first blister. Yeah, that was pretty amazing. It was pretty cool. Now it's just normal. I have really bony feet. I always bruise them on the floor when I'm doing splits or whatever because they're really bony.

*i/eye feel naive, what is she telling me*
*about dancing—is pain normal? cool?*

Well, that's what keeps me wondering about why, why? I wonder, and all I could think about is those practices. I mean, obviously, there's wonderful things that happen with dance, but I look at your feet, and I'm thinking isn't this interesting. Because it's pain that like, you say, is a part of it but on the other hand, is it…

Well, sometimes you.

Is it acknowledged?

Oh, definitely. It's like, and I mean teachers are like "Oh, yeah. We've been through it. We know what you mean but keep going babe. Too bad. We don't care. We know." The thing is that they have to be stiff like that because, I mean, you've got to do it, however you feel you've got to dance and that toughens you and then the next time that pain isn't so bad and you move up to the next level sort of thing.

Yeah.

*I think of the damage I have done to my body, fractures, torn ligaments, sprains, and the damage I continue… writing is a sedentary life…*

*I have a back ache…*

*I am thinking of sports such as football and hockey where pain and injury limit athletes' careers, those bodily reflexive practices, perhaps, ignored? Learning to dance/live with pain?*

*I think about the work of Miller (1990) and her ideas about poisonous pedagogy, those reproducing practices that keep the story going even when the practice of abuse continues: "It happened to me and I survived," or "it made me the person I am" position.*

*I remember my running years with a track club. I experienced leg and lower back injuries. Even with that pain I can remember hearing my track coach ranting at me "Hedy you're meek!" I hated him. I continued to train, doing hills, stairs and laps, regardless of the damage and abuse.*
*Was I toughened? If so, for what?*

And I mean, physically you're so deadly tired, but you have to really push yourself. Sometimes I sit in class and I'm like "why do I even bother?" I've had a bad week for that.

*"Why bother." I ran for him for 2 years. Then I quit and ran for myself.*

And so what keeps you going? Who keeps you hopeful and your story going?

Well, I think even just seeing other dancers around, you think and somebody else will say, "Oh they're so good. Oh my God! They're in advanced class. You know, they're so good." But I have to stop and think, but I can do that. I know I can. It's just that you realize, I haven't been pushing myself, and you've got to take it a lot into your own hands. You've just got to want it.

*Just seeing? What is seen?*

*How do we acknowledge girls and recognize what they know?*

Yeah.

*Why do we push ourselves to accomplish what we want, alone and in relation, and how do we live out the contradictions of the desire and the reality?*

I don't know. I don't even know where I'm going with it yet. I just know that I want to, I'm trying to discover what my limit is, and I guess what's most frustrating to me is because of my knee situation right now and I had a bit of tears on Saturday in class just because I was like "oh! enough" and it catches up with me every month or so and I'll be fine and you know everybody is going along and, "Yeah, I can't do that, you can't do those jumps." Okay, I'm okay with that, but every

*Gaah, there are days I don't know where I am going, learning to live ambiguity.*

once in a while, it just grabs you when they are specifically picking on one thing because teachers will sometimes do that, you know, we're really going to work on turnout today. We're really going to work on jumps. We're really going to work on heads, hands, you name it, because everything is important but I don't know. It will just catch up and I'll be like "Oh, God!" I can't even tell what my limit is because I can't jump through a whole class or anything without totally damaging myself.

*I feel the sadness of her story, of striving for perfection, pain for beauty. I think of living with injury upon injury that deplete my body of spirit and energy. But, on the other hand, I think about Maeve saying, "monthly," perhaps a body rhythm that ought to be integrated.*

*It's okay to be tired.*
*What will Maeve do when she teaches?*
*Without totally damaging*
*What leads girls to deny and damage their own unique physicality?*

Oh. Well, the knee pictures, that story makes sense.

Yeah, yeah.

I know, okay.

This one I took of me. I was impressed how it worked it and I'm always shocked how white I look. I mean do I look that white to everybody else? Holy cow!

*How do others see us? How do we see ourselves?*

That's just wild.

Freaky. This is just to illustrate how dislocated my right knee. How it actually is.

Oh, again.

*Although I am not so naive to think sport doesn't involve injuries, I wonder about the amount and degree of injury and pain. Who is watching the dancers?*

Look at it. Look how crooked that is. Okay, it's supposed to be there.

(Moves chair.) You can't really see but my knee is over there and it should be over almost that much more to make my leg straight.

*I don't have knee injuries, so I listen carefully. I also see women friends who live out knee injuries from earlier sport injuries.*

Yeah.

And so that way to keep my knee over my foot, which is what you have to do in ballet or you're just going to wrench everything.

So, what do they do? Is there anything that they can do?

It's like for that, I just don't have that much turn out in that leg it means. It just means that it's way more of a struggle to hold the turn out because I have to turn out from my hip.

So much pain. All I could think about was pain seeing these photographs.

*She's just got so much pain this "poor" girl.*

I figure that it's just a central point in my life, but they've been actually really improving lately. Really doing very, very well. I'm impressed. I was jumping today, and I've been jumping more and more. So that's good. (Dog barks)

*The ending, on the other hand. Maeve dances with a glad heart. She tells me often.*

I love it. I like them. There's my knee brace.

Oh, I know. This was another that I was "ooouu." This looks sore.

But there's a happy, there is a happy end on it. My foot. I like my feet. I

have good arches, even though
they're flat as pancakes.

*Implosion...*

Yeah.

When your feet can really bend.

Okay.

So that's okay.

Okay, let's stop this.
Okay.
Oh, it's going to stop on its own.
(end of tape)


## RETELLING MAEVE'S STORIES

I write about our conversations of Maeve's cameraworks as seeing in the dark and hiding in the light, learning to see in the shadows. Inside space is pushing outside light, a white and black dualism, perhaps a shadow of Maeve's sense of becoming a woman. I think about the body consciousness and what is concealed at the intersection/crossroads of becoming a woman. When I hear Maeve's wonders, I remember and think about the experiences of girls.

Maeve's repeated shots of already existing ballet photographs made me think about reliving wonderful experiences, and she told stories of a very connected group of dancers and I sensed her desire to reestablish and sustain pleasure while relooking at her ballet photographs.

I see Maeve's cameraworks as an expression of a body consciousness experienced through the intersection between historical representations of the human figure and the contemporary body politic. In my view, Maeve's camerawork poses the question: how do we open up the gender categories of "girl" and woman so that girls' identities, their self-constructions and activities, are not bound by rigid, exclusive gender standards constructed by both children and adults? How can girls claim gender, act out gender, and be unconstrained in their gender identities? Likewise, the other girls ask, how can girls claim desire, act out desire, claim pleasure/express pleasure, touch and be touched?

morgan

morgan

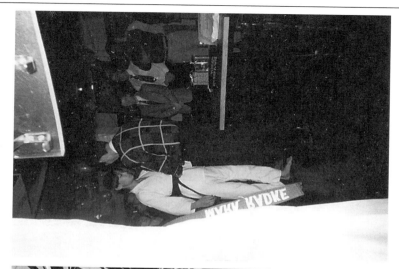

morgan

# THIS IS HOME

Morgan (94-12-02)
Cameraworks I
Projective project

This has got to be my favorite, I love
it so much. The sunset and the lake.
This is Calling Lake; we went there
would be a few months ago. It was a
weekend, two days. I went with
Beth's mom; she drove Beth, Jackie
and myself. So we went and we had
such a blast. It was so fun; it was on
an Indian Reserve, and it's just a
small town of people, and we were
all there with a bunch of Beth's
friends from Calling Lake. Beth
grew up there in the summers. This
is the cabin we stayed in; well, this
was not a cabin it was a nice beautiful house. It was beautiful. It was so
big.


Yeah!



Like those ones. The cabin's on
Pigeon Lake.




Oh, yeah.

*Beautiful, what is beautiful? To
whom?*


*Many of these cabins are homes.
I grew up by lakes in British
Columbia. As an instructor, my father
had 2 months of holidays each summer.
I had wonderful summers, times of
pleasure. Morgan reminds me of the
taken-for-granted in my life.
Morgan tells me about her learning at
home, gardening, cooking, reading,
drawing…and I find myself awake to
learning at home, what Bateson
(1994) writes of in learning as coming
home.
I think of Morgan's visual narratives:*
Discovering connections and regu-
lates within knowledge you already
have is another kind of homecom-

ing, a recognition that feels like a glorious game or a profound validation. (p. 205)

You didn't feel like you were tenting it out in the wilderness. It was enjoyable, and it's actually Beth's dad and stepmom's house, and they let us use the place. Normally they rent it out, so they let us have it for free. It was really nice of them. Already equipped with some food and you know munchies and stuff. So that night we roasted our food over the fire and our hot dogs and it was so fun. That was the last night we were there. It was the last sunset we saw and it was huge. You could see the entire thing, you know, no city buildings to block the way. It was lots of fun. That was a time when I was really stressed in school, so getting away was really needed.

*Where do I get away from it all? Morgan speaks about school stories and her underrating of surviving in them. She reflects on what she learned (often with her mother) and has turned a* "strange context into a familiar one, and finally into a habitation of mind and heart" (Bateson, 1994, p. 213).

Those day trippers can be good.

We went there for two nights: Friday to Sunday.

Weekends are better, no doubt. Just to get out of the city is what you're saying. I find sometimes when I do that. If I take just like a whole Saturday. Sometimes just go to an auction and drive out somewhere.

I like to get out of the city sometimes. I love the city, I grew up here
for the first 5 years 6 years of my life,
on Jasper Ave. I loved to sleep to the
sound of busy traffic. I loved it so
much then, but when we moved out,
I got used to the silence. And now
I'm back in the downtown for high
school, sometimes it's just too much
for me. I feel rushed when I'm
downtown by all the noise. Really,
I'd rather the quiet, but not too
quiet. So if I could get away anywhere, because when I was down
there in the West End, it was a bit
too quiet, so coming downtown was
a break. Something that was different. When it was too quiet, noise
was a vacation. When it was too
loud, quiet was a vacation. But now
since I'm used to both I just like to
get anywhere now. Does that make
any sense?

Sure.

This is one I took when I went down
in the ravine by the Bluebird river in
the West End, and I took pictures of
trees. Nothing more, just trees.
When they were developed, I went,
I showed some friends at Tai Kwon
Do and some of the students, and
they're like "Whoa. Were you sight-
seeing or just a tourist at Banff,
Jasper." I just happen to like trees,
and they put me down because of it.
They didn't understand me. Really I
think, trees are beautiful. All the
branches, I mean it's something I

*I have a sense of comfort when I talk
with Morgan. She tells me about philosophy books, world religions, and
international law that deserves attention. I think about what I should read
when I am with her.*
*I grew up in the same house and moved
to Vancouver when I was 18. Moving
out on my own, at least for a while. I
think about the noise of urban life and
how I make sense of my place. I love city
lights and dark silence.*

*I think about our pace of life in relation
to economics and different ways to live
my life. What matters?*
*I am reminded of the girl's struggles to
make images, of not wanting to waste
film, of capturing something not
expected, of wondering what I wanted....I wonder who they show
their photographs to.
sight seeing...*
*Morgan's film always had photographs
of trees, and she gave me a poem from
QC, 1995:*

TREE
Sitting on the earth, looking up at
the sky,
I notice the intricate design of his
arms.
Hundreds of them intertwine to
form a mystical masterpiece of art.
My eyes slowly run down his neck
and follow his long body down to
where I sit on his toes.
His coarse, rugged skin is upon my
back, and the animals are upon his.
With closed eyes I listen to the
music of the wind

would like to draw, but it would be too complex for me, like that's a pretty detailed picture.

rushing and blowing through his
wings.
Even standing at a distance I am
taken by his beauty
His strength so
overwhelming,
his color
peacefully blinding.
He's dancing like the sun,
and protects me
like an angel.
Sitting back down
on the earth,
once again looking up into the sky,
I can see my friend smiling with
me.

And when I saw it I thought this is something I would do. It's wild.

I love it. It is abstract.

Its nice because you could work like with a dark paper and just do the highlights. Like streaks of white, the positive, negative stuff. So what sort of feelings does it give you?

That's yeah, I'm just going....

Does it give you feelings.

I don't know I'm very bad at expressing feelings because to me they're too deep. And really there's no words. Like if I'm making love with someone, there's no way I would ever express it by just saying I love you. It's never enough. For my mom there's no way I could ever express how much I love her and show all

*Will photographing her experiences unearth possibility for Morgan to express her emotions? Can she picture a way?*

my gratitude and tell her how proud I am of her. I mean she is the most coolest person I know. She's got all the strength in the world. She's raised three kids by herself tragically. Like I mean we all came from different fathers. Long story but right now she's writing this book. She's got her own TV show. She's promoting her book on a local talk show and the CBC and it's in the bookstores. Ring the bells and all that kind of stuff. She wants to get us through extra curriculum activities. She's got us all into Tai Kwon Do; she protects us and has us in self-defense.

A unique woman.

I am proud of my mother, and I think she is the strongest because she is a survivor and that's how, probably, I learned to understand the abuse she experienced. She educated us. That's what her book is about. She educates people to try and stop the violence and so she teaches us that way. If I ever get into a relationship with a man who abuses me, he's out the door. That's the kind of stuff I've learned. To be strong in myself, with strong roots. And maybe that's what the tree signifies. I always thought

*I was interested in hearing Morgan tell her story about her mother in our first conversation, I was also thinking about what she sees everyday as she watches her mother.*
*I think a lot about protecting children. As a mother I watch over/with/ against my daughter and we are in Uechi Ryu karate class for self-defense. This was a very conscious decision. This matters to me, as I think and see the violence against....*

*Learning as coming home...has meant being a theorist of my own experience. And I think about my survivor story and wonder, has it made me stronger?*

*Stop the violence...*
*Who learns from the survivor?*
*I think of the secret secret story. When do women name the unnamable and tell the telling stories to their children?*

of it as life, and its branches are the many different paths of life. And there's just like life, it's so complex, so many different emotions, but yet it still is so beautiful. I mean, I know kids who wanted to commit suicide, and like why. I guess if you come from a certain background it will really affect you, of course it would affect you, if you're abused of course you don't want to live that long. I just want them to see the beauty of life that I do. I'm lucky enough to have a normal childhood so far. I love black and white photography a lot more than I love color. It's the trees even though it's in color it's still black and white with the sky, you know.

*beautiful as too horrid—but neither can it be denied; the horror has it own attractions*

*powerful*
*ever-elusive*
*ever threatening*
*a potential danger*

*picturing death as a way out*

*What is normal?*
*I had a wonderful girlhood…at home. I struggled to make other contexts familiar. I live with contradiction. I think of the tree roots/branches/ grounding/family. Learning along the way from abuse…so did I.*

What do you like about black and white photography? These issues came up at the university, some of my colleagues have been asking me. Why black and white? Find out what it is that the girls like about black and white photography.

*I think about how black and white is steeped in documentary photography, the photograph as evidence, austere, cold, objective. These are real photographs of the real thing:*

Well, I say it's best because there's no room for stereotyping. Like with that photo I took of those girls with the dyed hair, you wouldn't be able to tell they had bright colored hair, so you couldn't condemn them for being weak, as society often does to

Paradoxically, the black and white system signals what is real. It is the system for photographers to proclaim their intention to have their work and the issues it raises taken seriously. Black and white has be-

rebellious teenagers. Through my eyes, I don't know, black and white gives more feelings for me even though colour has more diversity and detail. In speaking of colour it's assumed there should be more feeling because red is encouraged as strength and blue as sadness. I don't see it that way; I actually see black and white that way, with the different shades.

Okay.

Like, the deeper the shade, at least to me, the more precise and strong it is. And the more it has an edge to it, the more feeling. And the light here, just the white skies, are more inviting, so when you put them together it's like very neutral comforting, you know.

Umhm

I don't know, I never have been asked the question before.

NO, no I mean they asked me and I thought, I just asked them. I'll ask them, is that what I said, I didn't know for sure. I mean to me there's a sense of timelessness with the black and white. When I look at black and

come the real system, the system of high contrast, the colours of confrontation. (Hebdige, 1988, p. 33)

Conventional namings—blue suggesting the blue of the sky, for instance—but also to the unconscious, that aspect of being which resides outside of the boundaries of the world we can name with language and thus think about, and, "as a result, color coded pictorial distribution." (Hebdige, 1988, p. 220)

*I have never asked, but the girls talk about loving black and white, and I think about the ethical issues surrounding colorization that converses black and white in a colored scene. I have struggled with this within my work, the transformation of color to black and white, and the costs of representation and technical challenges.*

white it reminds me of my babyhood.
I look at pictures of Chloé that I have
done in black and white. It's hard to
see a difference; I guess that's what I
like about it. It takes away from dating
generations.

But anyway, I was in the Library and
I saw this book, and it was just an
amazing book, I don't know, the
photographs were mainly of natural
things, rocks, cliffs and whatever.
There was a this one photo of a rock
that wasn't wet and a rock that was.
And how even when it's in black and
white, you can tell it's just the
smoothness of one that is wet and
you can see the definite layers of
what isn't. Black and white photography relies heavily on texture,
shadows and contrast to tell a story
and to relay the same information
color would. It makes it more interesting, you know. They had a picture
of people in this book I got, and the
thing is they had dark skin shows,
but it wasn't the first thing that hit
you. You feel like there's no racial
difference; people are people, you
know. With black and white there is
no colour difference, no discrimination, just simple truth.

*No difference...*
*i/eye am what i am.*
*I think about bodies*
*a some body*
*every body*

I see it. I never thought about that.
But you have all said that. I think it's
interesting; all of you have said I want
to do black and white. So I think that
interesting how others say that.

I've got this huge book, with portraits of actors from the 30s, 40s and the 50s. Its got pictures from Clark Gable to Garland and you know all these beautiful people, and they are in black and white, a really soft filter for that smooth look. You know it's almost as if they are all wearing the same thing.

*beautiful*
*between light and dark*
*clarity and obscurity*
*pleasure and pain*
*irritation and desire*

Yeah.

Beauty, their beauty extends more. You're not condemning them for, "oh look at the dress she's wearing" or "look at the colour of eye shadow she's wearing," you're just looking at the actual beauty that comes out. Well, I don't know, I just thought of it now.
Okay, let's go on here.

*beauty*
*beautiful*
*What is beautiful*
*Beautiful as a Victorian ideal, that of soft, smooth, delicate, harmless—or a more disturbing form of the elevated*
*imposing/inspiring/lofty*
*majestic/noble/outstanding/stately*
*virtuous*

(next photograph)

morgan

morgan

morgan

## OUR FATHERS

Morgan (95-01-27)
Cameraworks II
Making metaphor

*In this camerawork I suggested the girls think about making metaphors. Here we talk about working with self-portraits.*

What I was trying to do here was to make a self-portrait in the mirror, without a flash. I was thinking more artistically than what it really meant. So I am glad it turned out. It is really weird the way I got this doll in the shot; it was given to me by my grandfather who passed away. It's a really long story, but mom's father was abusive. For the longest time I adored him, not understanding he had been abusive, but he was a real wonderful man after he had gotten over it. He realized what he had done to his kids and from then on he had been a nice man. I met him a few times and we spent some time together. He gave this doll to me at Christmas or something, I forget what holiday. For some reason I've had it with me all the time. Even now it's still in my room. I called her Cindy and I thought it was weird because I was trying to take a picture of me, but I got the doll instead. I don't know I think in terms of, well, I don't believe in coincidence so

*My eye caught the doll; it reminded me of my Grandfather who had given me a doll at the train station in Holland.*

*A nice man...I wonder*

*My Grandfather was a fairly unknown person in my life. I never knew him. I only heard kind stories of him "spoiling" my mother.*

*What do I say?*
*Coincidence or meant to be? I wonder why the girls take the pictures they take. I think about the ones they choose to talk about with me. I think about what Judy Weiser told me in her workshop:* "You'll get information quickly." "You'll know what to do with it, you'll know where to go with it."

Okay.

And that's in my room. I am in the basement, and I only use curtains as walls.

*Bedrooms are spaces the girls have many stories around.*

That's your room in the basement.

*I had a room in the basement.*

Yeah, its cold and everything down there.

*Mine was warm.*

Yeah, really, you've got warm blankets?

No, I don't, I've got a few blankets but its fun. I was looking through this before. There are two pictures I made and I only used candle light. But ultimately they didn't turn out. And those are the ones I really wanted to see.

*What don't we want to see?*

Okay.

So it is a true self-portrait that in front of the mirror. I look dazed, weird.

*I saw the eyes.*

*the similarities*

Yours looks so small.

I think there's a lot of dust on the mirror, but I realized after I took this roll of film that I was going more for experimenting with the camera and the artistic side than what the pictures were supposed to be about. I just felt I was missing the purpose of it.

*Have I contributed to her feelings of constraint?*

I think each of you has found what it [cameraworks] means for you. We won't know what it all is until we sort of put a lid on it all. I'm not sure, right now, I don't have a sense of that at this point.

You see after that I thought and realized that my pictures were just pictures. I wanted to actually put some meaning in it. I was trying too hard for a minute. Here I was comparing because I have two fathers. One step and one natural, but this man's name is Daniel, and he's an exprofessional ball player, for the LA Dodgers and Milwaukee Brewers. From the time I was born he was pretty much there for me. He legally adopted me as my stepfather, and he was there for about 5 to 8 years. At 5 they got separated; at 8 years they got divorced. So now I haven't seen him in 5 years but he still pretty much raised me. And then he abandoned me; he was a very controlling man and he couldn't control anyone. So he just gave up and left, and my mom didn't want him around in our lives because he wasn't a helping man. He was manipulative, controlling, and he wasn't a very family oriented man. He had other families that he's abandoned. But I had...

You mean when you were younger he was...

*I have had a father in my life, all my life. Just the other day he wrote me a 4-page letter. My father writes words he has a hard time saying. I listen when Morgan tells me her desire for a father.*

*"Control" is a cultural story heard over and over again, again, and again, over again...*

Oh, he was great, for a kid you know. He gave me everything, it was more material stuff he gave me, everything I needed. If you needed like coats, you know, shoes, new wardrobe, if you had to go places, activities after school, it was great, but he was always at work, you know. So he would try to make up for it, and we would always go to the Bedrock Amusement park.

I don't know about that.

It was, like a fair ground, it was like being at Bedrock on the Flintstones. And it was really fun. I remember going there. We also went to Banff; he was a really rich man, wealthy. And so he pretty much raised me and this is another comparison of me and my real, my natural father, who I only met in Grade 4. And he decided not to be a part of my life when he found out I was born. When my mom left him she didn't tell him that she was pregnant until after. In Grade 4 I met him, and he seemed like a nice man. He had polio when he was young, and I mean, to me, those kinds of things don't bug me. Beth's got the fake leg and I didn't notice till like the next week when I saw her again. Then I realized she had a fake leg but I never thought of it before. Same with Andrew, I mean I knew he had a disability when I spent a week with him, but I'd never seen him before

*What does fathering look like?*

*Fair ground…*
*I think about Fred and Barney and their wives Wilma and Betty. Images of relationships, their dreams and fantasies and the lived script.*

*a natural father*

*I wonder if we ever really author our lives?* Then "this process relies on a structure of recognition by the individual of herself as the subject of ideology which also is a process of misrecognition. It is misrecognition in the sense that the individual, on assuming the position of subject in ideology, assumes that she is the author of the ideology which constructs her subjectivity" (Weedon, 1987, p. 30).

*What do girls notice?*

because he lived in Victoria all my life. He came to Edmonton to visit me the first time and we spent a week together and it wasn't till after that I realized that this man had polio, and he's got braces and he is restricted. He can't run, you know, he's not the kind of father, the typical father that a kid wants. I can't play soccer with him, you know. But he is still a nice man, and it doesn't bother me; I don't feel that there's any kind of a problem. So that is the last time I saw him, and then he finally told his family about me. His family never knew about me until I was about 12, or maybe I was about 13. I started to communicate with his family in England, and it is kind of, it's really stressful because having two fathers and both of them are not there for me. I don't know what these men think. I know it's not all men, but they just come and leave, they come and go. You know even if there's children involved they still go. Maybe that's the problem they don't want to come, but I talked to him just recently and sent him a really, really long letter and I didn't get a response. I explained everything, you know, why weren't you there, I want to have a relationship with you, I don't feel like you're my father and I don't want to call you dad, but I want to get to know you so that I can. But I never got a response, just a Christmas card that said, "How are you doing?" So he didn't get it or he's ignoring it. I didn't know who I am, that hurts a bit.

*What matters to them?*

*How do fathers play with their daughters?*
*What do fathers watch with their daughters?*

*How might those with authority and positions of power include their stories?*

*Response...*

*What counts? What matters? What does it feel like?*

*Hurts...a bit*

*and I think about her hurt
and her father's hurt.
Can I assume he feels pain?
How might Morgan understand this
story?
What can I say?*

You wonder how painful it is for him
to…

**I made an effort, I reached out
and…**

*What to say…*

But maybe that's why, you're so honest. You're so honest maybe that was
just too much.

*Honesty is a virtue, so I was always
taught at home and at church. I think
about being honest; living out stories
with integrity; being sincere; being
fair; being just; how does that look?*

**But then what can we do. If no one's
honest, then it's not going to go anywhere. Nothing's going to happen,
and I mean I have, I'm almost 16,
you know and nothing's happened. I
don't have a father in the right sense.
There's no right sense and there's no
normal kind of father, but there's a
certain kind of male figure that we
need to be influenced by. And I
never really had that. My mother is
very open, and she allowed these
men to come and go. She didn't want
me to be strictly mom's little girl
never knowing any of the fathers or
just restricting me, never to see
them. She allowed me to experience
and to get to know these men and
then to decide for myself rather, she
was very open very, you know, it
would hurt her to see me get hurt. At
least I'm not hurt in the sense of
never having known. So I just
thought it would be neat to take pictures to compare my fathers, you**

*What is a normal father?
What is father?*

*Morgan speaks openly. I hear a tone of
voice that questions while trying to for-
give. When can girls let go?*

*Do girls let go of their fathers?*

*Morgan has conversations that illumi-
nate stories of abuse; the evaded that
matters for her mother is shared.*

know. See I've been told that I'm like him, my natural father. I also have been told I look like him. I'm glad those turned out. And again that's in my room, in the basement.

This tells another story in research, too, with daughters and fathers, and where dads are, you know.
I don't know.

You know I mean you both are very…

Just recently I tried to get a hold of Dan, my stepfather; he lives in the city. He has decided to leave us alone because that's what we wanted. It was too stressful for my sister who is his natural daughter. She has gone through a lot. A lot of problems that she had to deal with, with him. Leaving, then coming and going, whatever. When it came to Christmas, we would go over there, and we would have to open up presents one by one, at the same time, there were no inequalities, it would be equal, right? But when I was done mine, she still had 10 more, and I felt there was a favoring thing going on because she was his natural daughter. She got more. She got a fur coat; she got a whole wardrobe at his house for whenever she visits and I didn't. And then when he went to the lawyers and said, "I would like to see my daughter." There was no plural in there. So it really hurt, and I finally phoned him one year and I, and it was good that I phoned

*Wow. Thoughtful and planned out. I am uncertain how to respond.*

*oh well,*
*I press the story into a space where I feel safe. Talk about the research.*

*Why would she? But I shouldn't assume to know.*
*Morgan has more photographs.*
*She holds these with care.*

*Christmas has such family ties; images of romantic notions of family are illuminated everywhere.*

instead of writing a letter because I think writing letters are much easier for me and I didn't want that kind of mushy, sugarcoated letter. Because on the phone you have to wait for a response and it's more emotional and raw. So on the phone I talked to him and I explained my feelings and I got angry for the first time. And I stood up for myself and since then really we haven't spoken and so recently I was going to try and talk to him again. I phoned his office and I phoned him at work, I mean home. And he's out; I guess it's not meant to be right now. But I might be moving soon.

*Moving...*
*such a big job*

Oh, really.

In about a year or two, out of the city, depending it's just an idea. So I want to see Dan again before I leave town because I don't really, I don't want to have to grow up and think why didn't I ever do that, you...

*I think about Morgan's mother, packing and searching for housing as she strug-gles with attaining full-time employ-ment. I think about the un/paid and invisible work the girl's mothers are involved with in relation to their daughter lives.*

And you will be alone.

*I think about our daughter, as an only child, being alone*
*or lonely.*

Yeah.

Well, okay.

He's really old; he's like 64 now. There's a 23 year difference between him and my mom. So that he could die of old age before I even move. But, yes, so I don't know.

*64 is young.*
*I look at the people who I work with and see vitality and wisdom.*

*death—another evaded story.*
*When can we talk about death?*
*Only when it happens to us?*
*Is there a way to make sense of this life?*

When you talk about the letter writing, yesterday one of my friends was
talking about letter writing and how
it connects our souls, you know.

*My mother-in-law is dying of cancer. I*
*felt unable to say my thoughts aloud.*
*With suggestions from Ronna and Joy-*
*Ruth I began writing. I wrote her*
*every week until it became too*
*painful...to see through my tears...*

I also felt the same need to connect
with my natural father, Andrew. I
wanted to ask him all the questions
about why he decided not to be a
bigger part of my life, you know all
those kinds of questions. And
because I've only met him once in
my life, and he's still practically a
stranger, I didn't want to ask those
questions over the phone. So I
decided to write him a really long
letter explaining all my feelings and
stuff. I think it's easier on paper than
it is on the phone. I have to hesitate
on the phone and worry about what
I am going to say because if I say it I
can't erase it. And so on paper, you
know, you can revise it and make
sure you don't say anything that you
don't want to say and make sure it
sounds good and that you get the
right message across. But the other
thing is I'm dyslexic and writing is
even harder and the writing takes so
much time and a lot of effort and a
lot of feeling and if he did not get it,
which it is a very likely possibility,
I'm not about to write another one. I
don't have the energy and the will to
do it over again right now. It took

*Morgan thinks deeply about her con-*
*nections and how she sustains relation-*
*ships. I see her as mindful in her com-*
*munication. What do we learn from*
*strangers?*

*Erase it.*

me about a week of emotions to
write that.

Oh, wow you didn't photocopy it.

Oh, no of course not, that's too bad,
too. But I wanted to phone him and
say did you get my letter. But if I
phone him and if he says yes I did, I
don't want to talk about it on the
phone. I want him to write his emotions back and I like writing things.
But if he says no I didn't get it, I
don't want to have to explain over
the phone what it was about then,
you know. So either way I have to do
some explaining, but I just want to
find out whether he got it or not.
What can I do but, once it's been a
while, I'll write him again.

But you put your return address on it.

Oh, he knows how to get a hold of
me.

It wasn't just your feelings though.
Maybe it will take him a year to
write one. Maybe he needs, I don't
know, I'm not trying to make excus-
es for him.

No, it's like that...

But what if, I don't know, but you
probably struck a core, about real, is
what I bet you've done.

*I can relate to learning struggles. This
is an evaded story for me, for now.*

*Why would she?
she's not a researcher. Yet...*

*What can I say?
I listen closely
and encourage her.*

*I really don't know what to say, I sense
Morgan's pain.*

Well, I hope I did, I want to move on.

I mean how do you respond to some of that. You have opened up a conversation.

I gave him, I felt I gave him room. I had questions, I wrote down questions and then how I felt about the questions. So I let him know where I was coming from and I asked him in the letter to think about that. Or at least I wanted some kind of response I don't want to be abandoned again. But if that's what I have to go through I guess. The thing is in Grade 4 it was him, his moving toward me he took the step to get to know me and to meet me for the first time. And now it's too painful that he's contradicting himself because he made the step at first and now he's backing away, you know. It doesn't make a whole lot of sense to me. What if it is too hard?

It's really interesting how you talked about your father since today I was re-reading the book, *Meeting at the Crossroads*. In that book the author talks about fathers and the girls letting go of fathers and at the age that you're at. Strange, you had just showed me those two pictures and your fathers and whole story was about those issues. I thought, oh, this is just bizarre.

*I fall back into my comfort with research, assuring her she is normal, whatever that is. Her story resonates with the lives of other girls in my research and the work I read—stories of lives of abandonment and betrayal of relationships.*

*It's not. I wonder at the stages and ages that are written about girls. Is it coincidence or do the crossroads for girls occur at a similar age?*

Never letting go of fathers. I mean, it's weird because they seem to want to let go of me. Okay, Dan was there, but it was 5 to 8 years, and Andrew was there in Grade 4 for about a week, you know. That was his fathering period, and it's not that I'm letting go now. I was thinking that you don't really let go of your fathers. In my situation I guess when you're older, you know how you let go of parents, because you're older and you're growing up. For me, it is not a matter of letting go of even Dan; it is of being more independent and looking at it from a different perspective, about seeing him as man, not only a father. When I was a girl I really wanted one of my fathers to be there for me at times. Or there's things that I just wanted to talk about with things I wanted to know or I just wanted to spend time with this person, who was supposedly part of my family and helped create me. But he was never there, and so now I'm looking at it differently as two people who have a common bond, and I feel almost obligated to get to know him, at least just a bit. You know, for me I really don't know the man and my real father. And just to get to know him just a bit. Just to perhaps maybe one day of true bonding or something, just one set. And then from there on if we decided if we really don't like each other as people. Then we just, you know, do the Happy Birthday thing and

*I agree with Morgan, I never let go of my father, his image, his story, his influence.*

*Not really. I never let go of my parents, I mean I live apart, but the connection, herstory and echoes of parenting influence my meaning making. Of course, I make my decisions framed through what I've seen and heard over my growing up. Morgan's desire for a father, male influence, a nuclear family makes me think of stereotypical stories and images, those of good and right.*

*Those pictures shown on television and in magazines. Morgan's story is different as she questions experiences of bonding. I think about Miller (1984) in her book* Thou shalt not be aware *and her framework of being a child's advocate/witness.*
*What do girls witness?*

nothing more. Or maybe we're just totally separate, but I don't think you ever let go of your fathers. You're always bonded to them in some ways because, like my mom she was abused by her father but she still loved him and there's different kinds of feelings. I still love Dan, *Always love?* even though he was controlling and manipulative and put my mom through hell, you know. I still love him because of the times he was there for me when I was a kid and and because I felt that what he gave me was love and I wish I had that again. But he's changed and so have I incredibly, but... *Always change/changed/changing*

(dog barking at the door)

*a part of me thinks shit...*
*working in my home has interruptions*
*that stop the story*
Oh, there's Maeve. *just as they did while working through*
*school interruptions*
(end of tape) *time*
*for conversation*
*a need for fluidity*
*the story never ends*
*but on the other hand: it so nice to work*
*with girls in my home*

## RETELLING MORGAN'S STORIES

I found that Morgan's cameraworks challenged conventions of privileging beauty. What is beautiful? Who decides what images are beautiful? Her photographs lead me to associate the taken-for-granted in my life. Photographs of architectural fragments from the city in which she lives re/presents a sense of daily urban life. I see Morgan as a body who is grounded through her connection with nature as she shared stories of her love of trees, branches and the earth. These stories reflected her relation to family overlaid by place, home, and history.

Hearing stories of Morgan's family life conjured up stories of the place of fathers in my life as I restory my experiences of being the eldest daughter and a mother. I began to equate her hurt with an idealized form of family that creates a discomfort on my body. I see Morgan's images of her father of a time: a lost time; an impossible time in which she had dreamed of an idealized father-daughter relationship. Morgan's stories of her fathers remind me of the uncomfortable positioning and conclusions I occupy after seeing and hearing her stories. In hook's (1989) view, the realm of the personal can become politically efficacious and transformative and need not obscure the conditions of the production of experience if women do not merely "name" their experiences but also "place that experience within a theoretical context" (p. 110). I read Morgan's photographs and story telling that hooks (1989) writes "as a process of historization. It does not remove women from history but enables us to see ourselves as a part of history" (p. 110). Morgan witnesses experiences that are not bifurcated from theory, or as hooks (1989) suggests, "The act of speaking out can become a way for women to come to power" (p. 129). I write Morgan told stories with courage.

In my conversations with Morgan, I experienced a heightened awareness to the living out of photographic ethics involved in doing visual research with girls. Her sensitivity pressed me to look at my research relationships with the girls as friendships. Morgan's careful and thoughtful responses in sustaining conversations with myself reflected an honesty that grew with time. Her sincerity and questions of what it means to care in people's lives in relation to those who hold positions of power opened space for making the private public. Being with Morgan I think about response—of how I act and do not act in my research practice.

thya

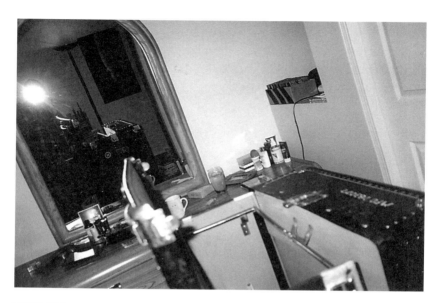

thya

thya

## WHEN THE WOLF LIVES IN YOUR HOUSE

Thya (95-01-04)
Cameraworks I
Projective photographs

Money, I don't know, its just kind of nice. Oh, another thing. I'm saving up for Europe. That's the first thing I want to do when I graduate from high school. I only have $300. I don't have a job, so that's a substantial amount. Considering it's babysitting money.

*Position to class.*

*Thya dreams of travel and she does.*

Yeah really.

*Girls' work, the labor of care. What work is available for girls? Is it meaningful work? I think of my girlhood employment, the work of fashion modeling, the economic equity of the work.*

I mean I'll have a job pretty soon.

*What sort of work would girls like?*

Are you wanting to work?

Well, I do because I need the money, but I really don't want to get a job. I am enjoying taking it easy before. I mean 3 years from now I will be working, and I won't quit until I'm 65. But I really want work, work that I will enjoy but not a job. You know, I just wish I could teach dancing. To me that's not a job. You know that's a dream. That is so wonderful. And I love kids, and I love ballet, so I can teach kids ballet. Yeah, and I am going to. Because this year I am finishing intermediate. I felt really discouraged because they tell you in the

*What images is Thya learning from?*

*Are we raising our girls to work, or are girls still accessories?*

*I know, I know what I want to do. I know doing what you love changes the work...but the institutional story haunts me. Love children, what does Thya mean?*
*teaching dance*

first 2 months about our new performances. You were so discouraged
and I would come out of class I
couldn't do anything; I vegetated all
summer. I went suntanning at
Queen pool. Like I wouldn't swim.
I'd just go there dip my feet in and
suntan, and I lost a lot of muscle
over the summer. Going back was so
tough. And I thought I would never
be able to do it. But I've been getting better and practicing in my
room before I go to bed. The other
night I was doing splits and sit-ups.
It's gotten a lot easier and I am
doing things much better. In fact, I
look a little like the prop students,
and I am saying I'm not doing too
bad considering they're here everyday and they're not doing that well.

And who are prop students?

Oh the prop students and company
students they go every day and it's a
full dedication. I was in the prop last
year, but this year I have 8 classes,
and I'm doing Math 20, Math 30,
Physics 20, Biology 30 and English
and Social and French. So I have all
these classes this year, so I thought
there's no way I can be dancing like
20 hours a week. So I am only dancing 5 hours a week. I am still doing
okay considering that I'm not training my body every day, because I
only dance Tuesdays and Saturdays.
But I mean even Maeve says I'm
doing pretty good. But she's in
"company," she's there all day, all the

*Who decides? Whose evaluation counts?*

*Thya is in a "gifted" program.*

*What does a "gifted" curriculum look like? I think of the artificial divisions as I look at the photographs and stories that girls' tell and retell, live and relive. There are spaces where attempts to integrate a greater whole occurs. I also think about the embedded stories that are held with superglue.*

time. And she says I am doing pretty good. When you're in "prop" or "company" you are there every day. But that doesn't mean anything.

Even when you work out every day?

*Who keeps our stories of believing in ourselves going?*

That's why there's so many, like if you saw the bodies on the dancers at my ballet school you would be like wow because they all have perfect bodies. Well so many of them have perfect bodies. And they're really good when you try because if you don't try because they get sick of it. Being there everyday. You know, I think they need a break.

*The perfect body....I/eye think about how foreign our bodies are.*

Well, don't they have other things to do?

If you are dancing too much and the majority of the people will just start to give up after a while. Because you don't start to notice the drastic improvement.

*Thya's camerawork is laden with ballet images of her body. Dana took a mini-narrative of her doing housework in her ballet clothes.*

Okay.

So you start to feel really discouraged sometimes.

*Can we learn from disappointment?*

But you made a decision then last year to focus on like school and academic stuff.

*Did Thya decide or was this presented to her?*

Yeah! And I want to do that, so next year I will only have 4 classes, and I can dance full time next year. And next year I'm going to get my teacher's certificate.

You have. Okay, so you have a plan?

Oh, I have plan, a real plan, and     *a Real plan*
next summer I am going to work all     *What is Real? Real for who?*
summer. And get money so that
when I finish next year I can go to
Europe, right after high school.

Well you probably applied for a     *Mother/researcher response*
dance scholarship, too?

I did, actually I applied for this year
and got one.

Good.

So half of my dancing is paid for.

Oh good.

Which is good because my dad said
he wouldn't pay for it anymore.

No.

No, he is not very understanding.
He said I can join anything else and
he would pay for it. But he was sick     *Is Thya being punished? And for*
of paying for ballet.     *what?*

Oh,

It was like, like little revenge. I do
know what the revenge was for. I     *revenge*
didn't do anything so that he just he     *an evaded story*
wouldn't pay for it anymore.

Oh really?

Yeah.

How many years have you been doing this.

**Ten.**

Oh wow!

**This is my tenth year. And my Dad hasn't really complained about paying for dance lessons before. But he thought I was just using it too much as my life, but actually I should be able to make my own decisions. If I felt comfortable doing things like that, last year, why not. I still do spend time at home. I mean not as much but, big deal, all he does is watch TV, when he comes home, you know. It doesn't really matter anyway, what am I missing. Certainly me and my mom are really good friends; she is my best friend.**

*What decisions do girls make on their own?*

*Beyond the pain of her particular story of "what am I missing" as a researcher I feel discomfort, as though I were eavesdropping on a painful intimate family scene.*

Yeah.

**But I mean my dad doesn't really, he's not in my ways, like.
And that oh,**

What's that on the television?

*We're looking at a photograph of Thya's television...changing the subject, looking at different images.*
*I feel awkward and confused in part because it's not that I haven't heard stories or read the theories.*

**Well, it's just some violent show.**

[conversation ends]

*just another violent show*
*I watch television closely.*

Thya (95-12-09)
Cameraworks III
Collecting culture

Okay let's finish these pictures, Christmas tree, the trunk story.

Oh, the trunk, that was where all my secrets are now. And then I just feel comfortable in ballet clothes because of low cut things and stuff. I feel comfortable wearing a bodysuit. Because you're running around usually all the players are in the bodysuit. And this one, this picture has I was sitting beside my trunk because that is where I hide all my essential things.

Yeah.

Like I keep all my secrets and my bond in there. I think my boyfriend took this one; he just asked me to look up, and he was standing on my bed and so this one was kind of a surprise, too. But this one wasn't. Oh, that's the trunk I got for Christmas.

Oh,

I really, really wanted one and we had to switch my whole room around because my dad snoops through my room. He does, he snoops through my room. And I wanted to hide all my love treasures in there. So I locked it always and

(I asked permission to show Thya's photographs for my first AERA poster presentation.)

*Each time I wanted to show the girls' photographs I talked with them first so that they knew I was making their cameraworks public.*

*Secrets, where are they hidden and are they secrets once told?*

*She has photographed herself in ballet clothes with a vacuum cleaner.*

*What stays private for Thya?*

*Cameraworks III meant risking... collecting culture was not the most liked project.*

hide the key. That is a neat present to have. I am going to paint it or something.

*I probably look surprized, like I don't want to hear this.*

What's your dad looking for when he goes through your room?

I think he does, I don't know what he's looking for. But I just come home and my clothes are sticking through my doors. Or my drawers are partially open. He does it to my sister. She had all her secrets written in her diary and my dad went through her diary so finally she would leave little notes saying dad you "scuzbucket" I know you are searching through my drawers. But there's nothing really for him to find because I hide things so well, like I have lots of stuff hidden in my room. I took it all and just shoved it in my trunk. So now he cannot see it.

I wonder if he's going to look for that key.

I have that hidden really well, too. There's a lot of places in my closet to hide things because it is so packed with junk.

*bedrooms…*

I never thought about that. I wonder if my dad went through my stuff in my room. You know, I would be surprised.

I don't know what it is.

Well perhaps dads do that to their
girls. Other girls have told me that. I
don't remember who it was though.
Her dad read her diary.

**That is so terrible.**

That's like sometimes Steve has said
to me, "Oh you can open it." But I'm
like, "No its addressed to you." I just
don't feel right looking.

*I think a lot about what private and
public means.*

**It is terrible, I couldn't, I would feel
so bad.**

Yeah, I wouldn't look.

*What don't we look at?*

**I'm so proud of that trunk that no
longer can my Dad go through anything.**

(end conversation)

thya

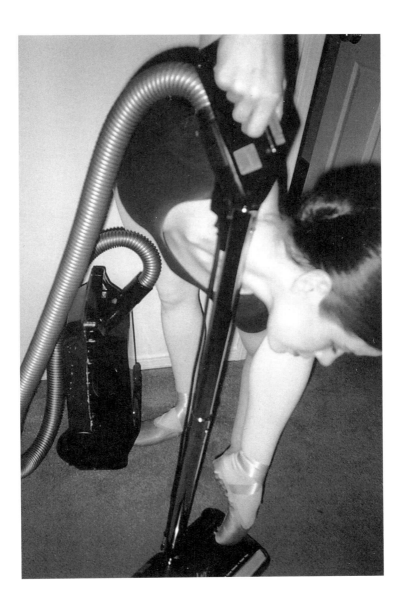

thya

thya

# MARRIAGE: THE GREAT CANADIAN DREAM

Thya (95-01-04)
Cameraworks I
Projective photographs

And they still love each other a lot and that's how I'm going to be when I get married. We're going to have kids. It works believe it or not. People don't think nowadays because 1 in 2 marriages break up but I don't know you find the right person...

*Desiring children...*
*What are our expectations for marriage?*
*I think of how marriage has changed since the turn of the century. Women's work and expectations in relationships.*

Hey I've been with Steve since I was 18.

*Who do we learn from? What scripts are absent?*

Yeah that's quality.

*Quality?*
*Who takes out the garbage? Who pays the bills? Who does the invisible work?*

But that's true. People don't talk about it. We hear always.

*The glossy view or the oppressive view. Thya likes to talk about marriage. So do I, not because I promote the ideology, but because I see girls desiring to author this script. I see adults ask girls and boys from toddlerhood on "So, are you married?" "Do you have a boyfriend?" We have created television shows that ask children those very questions and laugh at their responses. I believe we sell marriage in our culture through wedding stores, diamonds, and other stories. I wonder what happens to productive independent girls once they step up to the altar? What happens to their lives?*

The bad thing is that people give up so fast on relationships now. I mean it's weird because I still have friends from when I was 5 years old, and I'm still in touch with them. I mean, I don't know, people give up nowadays too easily. Like in relationships.

*But sex and relationship are different.*

Well relationships are a lot of work!

They are, but if you love someone enough to marry them then you should love them enough to work through most problems. I mean unless it's beyond fixing.

*What's beyond fixing?*

Abusive?

*What is an illustration of this abuse?*
*Are there identifiable signs, any visual signs beyond a network television image?*

Abusive.

I think you do go through impasses. I've been talking to some women friends who have been in relationships for a long time and then all of a sudden they don't really understand what's happening but I think that as you are in a relationship for a long time, you know.

*How should I talk about this with Thya?*

There is a cycle. That it's not uncommon. You just turn around…

*Perhaps it is disillusionment. Or finding out who you are. Finding our self with an other body for the first time.*

*What is common? From my perspective, my standpoint, my reading of the great Canadian dream.*

You just give up so easy. It's sad. Especially for kids, if there's kids in the family.

*Sometimes I think it's harder to give up.*
*It's hard to let go.*
*Ahhh the dreaded line of "it will hurt the children."*

I imagine it's hard.

*But hard can be better.*

It is. Especially when the parents become bitter, but if they stay friends, then it's okay.

It takes a real…

*REAL…Okay, what matters?*

It takes a real mature couple. I think.

Really.

If they stay human.

Without, you know using the children.

It's awful! And also it's sad when everything gets split up half and half. That must be the worst part.

I have two friends right now going through divorces. Before Christmas my one friend, I thought I was just like you know.

You want to hear it but…

It's so sad…

It is! This is…
(change the subject)

(In my third conversation with Thya, the story of marriage surfaces again. Partly because I ask, but Thya has also talked with me on the telephone.)

Thya (95-03-18)

And would you say, now you did say some thing's would be changing with Dana, too.

*Mature? What's mature?*

*I have watched intelligent "humans" do the most bizarre cruel acts postmarriage.*

*But I choose to silence that story. Would it be gossip? Or a telling story? We're spinning another story, out of my experience, I consider telling such a story but abandon the telling. I feel a sense of loyalty, respect for my friend and of telling her story of betrayal.*

*This is my projection and i/eye evade the sad stories, this is my first conversation with Thya.*

Well, we had a little talk about things, and I don't know, everyone keeps bugging me about am I going to get married to him. You would be surprised how many people ask me that. I mean I don't know because like I am 16. I don't know, I am so young. I know that I like planning ahead with certain things to do with my life, just my life. Not my life and someone else's, and he's planning everything for our life like, everything he wants to do he has to do with me because he wants to be with me. Which I don't like. I want him to do stuff for himself, and then I can have respect for him. Like he is going to a technical institution and wants to do that because he didn't apply to the University because he wants to do a 2-year program so that hopefully he can get a job right away so he can put me through university. Because I found out about student loans, and my dad makes too much money, so I can't get a student loan. But my dad refuses to give me any money to go school. So I don't know what I am going to do. So my mom babysits, and she is trying to save up money for me to go to university, and Dana wants to help, too. But I feel bad because I feel as if there is no money for what he wants to do. But he really feels that he doesn't wants to go to university right now because he want to go to the technical school. But right now he doesn't care about being well rounded; he wants to go into technology or something.

*MARRIED...*

*Who pays for our education? I think about economic parity. Who gets an "education?"*

*I reread my high school journal where I question myself: "Am I going to marry my boyfriend?" I wrote about not being able to live without him, but I have. Thya tells stories about Dana that*

*remind me of my highschool boyfriend,
adoring, cool, possessive, and figuring
out who he is in this romantic story. Is
Thya going from her father's house to
Dana's? Do girls experience life alone?
With other girls? Women? Men? What
are girls wanting from relationships?
Work, school, babies…I see threads of
my story. Babysitting, the labor of care,
the place of women's work. How does
what our mothers experienced affect the
writing of girls' life texts? Girls are
looking at…*

*I feel awkward "being well rounded"
Thya speaks about her mother's desire
for Thya to attain a University degree.
In several conversations she tells me
about economic struggles of her family.
Thya tells me Dana's mother raised
three children and went to university.
I'm thinking about puppy love, young
love, what are her notions of love?
Unselfish, yet Dana wants to "keep"
Thya. She already names the struggle of
being owned, objectified, used.*

Yeah.

He wants a job in chemical research
and engineering. I think, I believe
him, but still, he is very unselfish. I
feel so bad about that and I feel so
bad that my dad won't see him and
be nice. He makes a lot of money,
and he won't spend any of it on me or
university. My mom says you have to
make your own money because I
don't have any to spend on that. But
he goes and buys thousands of dol-
lars worth of computers and computer equipment. And he gets drunk
all the time. I might sound

selfish, but I don't think that's a real selfish thought to think; he could help pay for my education, you know, because really it is good for him, if his kids get good jobs. I would really love to go into medicine. I'll find a way though; I'll work longer and save.

*What sense is Thya making from watching her mother in this relationship?*

*I believe Thya will.*

You could get loans if you're not living at home, but that could even be tougher.

*Can Thya write or picture a way out?*

**I don't know if I could handle it.**

I don't know, it would be really hard.

**That is weird because now I need help. They're teaching how to live by yourself with your boyfriend.**

*An evaded experience, where do they learn?*

I did a university course. Part of the C.A.L.M. curriculum that was a computer simulation and we had to go through these experiences, both good and bad, and then things happened, for instance, now you had unprotected sex and you have an STD, or didn't pay the bills and now you've gone bankrupt, or now you had a baby because you both finished university.

**Oh, wow!**

*Later, the girls tell me about who teaches the C.A.L.M. class: "The teacher who hasn't had sex in 10 years, be real."*

Then the program provided points, happy points etc. and then you got half the points when you made it through a university degree. I remember enjoying this assignment.

As artificial as it was, it was fun because you got paired up with a person that you may not have chosen. I found it interesting to see how I figured things out when differing values surfaced in this arranged relationship. It was cool.

*Who teaches girls to love,*
*to love carefully*
*to learn about their body's mind*
*who they share their bodies with?*
*I find myself thinking about the erotic*
*and sensual film Kama Sutra that tells*
*another story of love and a historical*
*place of women in Indian culture.*

**Thya**
**Interview 3**
**Cameraworks III**
**Collecting culture**

*Thya addresses relationship experiences. Today I sense she is figuring out another dimension of her friendship with Dana.*

*It's been close to a year, and Thya is still in relation with Dana. In a previous telephone conversation, she tells me that her relationship is shifting and that she would love to talk.*

Do you think it is different? I don't mean to trap you, but do you think it's different when you are in a relationship that's been a long time now. I'm making an assumption. I don't even know if you want to get into that, you don't have to. But, I think about my own high school relationship, I was intimate with one person and now, today, I wonder how school friends name relationships. Particularly when you're with one guy for a long time, in the same intimate relationship. When

I was in high school you were teased for being "the tease" or "the slut." I don't know? Would it be same today?

*Could I be any more evasive myself? THAT. IT. I want to ask directly, but I'm skirting around the issue of what adolescents call each other when they're sexually active.*

That's what...

I don't even know if I am just talking off the top of my head.

I really do see what you are saying, but like girls, girls are so strange because, I do agree about that. Girls, often they show one thing but they're meaning another. But in my school it happens to be more that it is all right for a couple to be intimate if it's long-term. And if a girl sleeps with a guy after a date, a day or two not even a couple of weeks of going out. But then they're called sluts, and a guy isn't. Nothing has really changed but the trouble with my school is they sleep together but they have been going out for months and months, or years like in some cases. No one finds that weird; they just think it's like they're a married couple already. And they think they are ready.

*Don't we all...*

*I think of multiple truths, multiple meanings and multiple representation.
Will this symbol, sign, story, ever change?*

*girls are sluts and boys are not...*

*Married already
In an already interpreted world...*

Okay.

*Are they loving carefully?
Ideals of romantic love and a curriculum of fear...*

And treat them like a married couple, okay you know. Like our finances, we have saved money together, and it is in a bank account because we are going to Europe next year.

*Is this a sign of commitment?*

I was wondering how things were going with your boyfriend and if you were still planning on doing that.

It is serious, and I'm sure there is concern that I'm 16, and last year before I went with Dana when I was 15, it was so bizarre because we never imagined that a year from now I would be going on a little vacation with a guy and his parents, you know. Dana has spent the night at my house. I would have never guessed that I would be doing this, you know. But I never wonder what life is now, it has a lot to do with life before, like we are together all the time.

*I think back to how I dated the same boy throughout most of my high school years. We were serious, went away for weekends, and spent time with each others' parents.*

*Together all the time*

Okay, that's interesting.

I need Dana to keep him out because

*My boyfriends never stayed over night with my parents' knowledge.*

Oh, okay.

I don't know it was a couple of times when we were out he was just so nice to me. And the fact that before ballet he would buy me a gift, a bike fender. It just meant so much to me, like that he would think to buy that for me, even as small as it was, it was so nice.

I know, it's times like that, that always means to me and he still does. He is still very kind to me and then I think about people saying oh, you were so young and then I think, well I was young to people then, you, I mean I have been in relation for over 18 years.

*Naming my story of marriage*

**That's so long.**

Then I think there are good things, too. But we never explore those, we always just say what they shouldn't do, what they ought not to do. Not that they should tell you what to do.

*I find myself mindful to the telling of heterosexual stories, wondering how and where I name other stories of possibility. What is my culturally dominant and privileged position and how can I dismiss it as irrelevant? I wonder if Thya can be aware of other agents or her own agency, and thus how one posits a different perspective in the frame of the natural or universal vision of marriage?*

**That is true.**

Just interesting,

**I was glad that you guys have been together for so long.**

Yes, I guess I can't imagine my life without him, but I feel as though I had my own life within his life.

*I have deep feelings and love in my relationship.*
*What does Thya imagine?*

See that is so important.

*I can critique the heterosexual perspective of marriage. I also live a script independent of my partner, and I still trouble my script.*

I mean we have had highs and lows, but mainly not, we get along really well. I don't know, but I never think about, until I talked to you girls, perhaps, it is an age difference. Because I don't think about it anymore, what is age...

*I think marriage/cohabitation works for some people and not for others. Some grow together; there is no right time, age, place or space. Marriage is as Heilbrun (1988) writes, "If she marries, why does the marriage fail or succeed in the familiar roles of wife or husband, but because they have evolved, or failed to evolve, a narrative of marriage that will make possible their development, as individuals and as a couple. What does 'successful' marriage really look like? We have remarkable little evidence of the 'story,' as opposed to the convention, behind long marriages between women and men who both have established place in the public sphere" (pp. 27–28).*

I think about age, well I will be 17 in a few months, and if Dana and I are still together by the time I am 18, like really it is so hard to find someone that you do love, and someone that you get along with really well. Then when people say do you think you will be with Dana for a long, long time. Sometimes I say, yes it is a big possibility because all the guys I meet at school, none of them are even close to having trust in a girl,

*Hard to find someone to love*

*Trust in a girl... Trust in a woman...*

how cute I think he is, you know. It's like, like my sister who has been going out with, well she is married to Gary now, but they have been going out since she was 17. It's all you do for a 13-year relationship, and there are some people at school who don't even have anybody. And they seem so lonely.

*Lonely*

I know something has come out that I have been reading, Lonely.

*Learning to be alone in relation*

They are lonely, and all my girl-friends who never had boyfriends, they are like, you are so lucky to have someone you can count on. The reason I can get along so well with Dana is that I am strong enough in myself that I don't have to rely on him all the time. That's the reason that we're together so long.

*cheerleader vs. critic*

*Can there be independence within oppressive scripts of systemic discrimination?*
*In time?*

(Later in the conversation Thya tells me about her travel plans.)

I can't wait. It would be so real though to be in the same hotel room, you know cause when he stays at my house overnight "oh, goodnight" and I kiss him goodnight and I go off to my mom's room, you know. And then it would be oh, goodnight we'd be in the same room. I don't know what I'll do, I don't even know, and my mom she is happy for us that we are going to Europe.

*So Real.*
*What's real?*
*What does Thya experience as real?*

*Who encourages relationships with boys? The intimacy, entitlement, and freedom?*

That would be interesting, I just wondered about that, going away is fun.

That's why people say we seem like a married couple.

*I am remembering the times I was away with a boyfriend. The fun. The freedom. I wonder if I thought of myself as married? Or just as coupled? I always had a large circle of friends who illuminated the same stories.*

It does seem different, you're really intimate, it does seem committed, to say you are saving up.

*Images of intimacy. What are they?*

Especially it might be that we go, we might be going next year this time.

Right when you are finishing school.

*My educational researcher script, finish school for...*

Right when I am done cause I will be graduating that half year early. So when he has his spring break, we might go. Or what is this when they get a couple of weeks off. I don't know when that is but we planned it then because it is not the peak time.

*Dana is at the University, not in the Trade School program as originally planned.*

That is a good idea. I want to plan a winter holiday next year. I really want a winter holiday.

*I am fading, dreaming about leaving these harsh Western winters of 30 below and piles of snow. Winters are dark and long. Images of leaving are conjured up easily.*

I do, too.

To get away when it is minus 30.

And if it doesn't work out, then we will go to Mexico. It isn't as an expensive a trip, but I'm already thinking Mexico is a warm place to go and just relax. But I really want to go to Europe to see things.

Yeah.

*She goes to Europe with Dana.*

You know, I don't want to have that
more of a married person vacation,
you just go and relax and lay on the    *A "married person" vacation*
beach and stuff. That's not what I
had in mind.

You want to go and do things.

I want to go and do actual things.
Like spend time looking around. I
don't care if I don't have much
spending money.

Sorry I we'll need to turn this off.

*Several months later in a telephone call
after returning from Europe Thya tells
me she is no longer seeing Dana. They
have broken up. And Dana has shown
her his disapproval of the breakup by
following her, showing up at places
where she is and making telephones
calls asking forgiveness. Thya tells me
"No way" she's over him.*

## RETELLING THYA'S STORIES

In recalling Suleiman (1994), *Risking who one is: Encounters with contemporary art and literature*, I think of Thya's photographs of "party life" as glimpses of a past into abject girl teen life. Stories of boyfriends, first loves, and marriage continue. Seeing this, I wonder as a researcher and as a mother about how I write on the body of marriage, knowing "traditionally, men belong to groups, to society (the matrix, the canon). Women belong to men" (Brooke-Rose, cited in Suleiman, 1994, p. 169).

Thya's stories remind me about tensions of wanting to belong. What do girls belong to? What do I belong to? Thya was a dancer of 10 years, active and productive in a subculture. What stories are reproduced? Marriage? A room of one's own? How would I teach girls to love carefully within institutional spaces of learning? What stories do women tell? What is left silent? Ignored? What continues to be institutionally dismissed? How would I know which students live within/through/around stories of abusive practices? What is seen? What is told? What happens in girls' search for self in relation to authorities, in particular, those who want control of their limited position? I see Thya speaking to disturbing trends that sustain the containment of girls in an attempt to control activities and desires.

# And Then Some

In researching girlhood, I see that the effort of asking critical questions is at times frightening and almost impossible and may not always produce the desired results. Yet those questions need to be asked, if not at the moment, later, not lost to social mandates that eclipse experience in strict ideology or dominant notions of self. What are the socially inscribed controls on the body? How are these boundaries personally negotiated? How do we play a role in their enforcement and redefinition? These notebooks and visual narratives are passages, moments cracked open by the senses, perhaps seen as naive and analytical acts of memory and imagination.

I have woven Beth's, Maeve's, Morgan's and Thya's experiences throughout these stories as a way of composing visual narratives that speak of girlhood pleasure and violence, dis-ease, disappointment, love, depression, self-loathing, and transformation, as a space of possibility to recast self and see the evaded within the lives of these girls. Questions remain:

Who has the authority to speak?
Whose identity is sanctioned?
Whose experience is universalized?

I have attempted to address moments when language, photographs and "self" suffer categorical rupture. Our work is inventive and lies in the realm of the writing on the body. Our work is our truth.

## AND THEN SOME

> what does it mean
> "and then some?"
> please say more

**And then some**

**Beth**

Beth "loves what I wrote," although she tells me, "I do tend to go on and on about Tori." She and a friend have read our words and, for me, provide a narrative affirmation. Her read of her stories matters. On the telephone, I tell Beth about my draft deadline being pushed up and finding a sense of completion with the work. She assures me, "You'll get it done." It is "great." Beth's optimism is appreciated. I want the girls to love what I have put together. I hope they see a narrative truth for themselves and that I remain seen as a friend. This matters to me.

In February I wrote a reference letter for Beth for a film school. She was accepted, and she is moving to Vancouver. I think about my life in Vancouver and feel her excitement. We are trying to have a little get together before she leaves. And I wonder, will I see Beth again? I will give her my address and a self-stamped envelope. I will miss Beth's humor and energy. I sense her sadness about having to leave close friends and her wonders of changing cities. Beth has shaved off her hair, sold her sports car, and quit her job, moving on. Beth's mother is moving to Florida, and Beth tells me she wonders about her place called home. She thinks about what will be left here for her. I sense her loss. Looking at her bedroom photograph, Beth smiles remembering her bedroom, now dismantled. She begins a new chapter in her life. She will be sharing a space with a friend, a boy that Maeve knows from school. Hearing this, I sense a security for Beth, that of being in connection with a friend. Going to film school is a dream come true for Beth.

**And then some**

**Maeve**

Maeve reads her stories and relooks at her photographs, those we selected over the 3 years. Today, however, at the table in my house drinking licorice tea, Maeve tells me she has a cold and allergies and that she is not feeling well. We are looking at the cameraworks and stories, which Maeve has not seen in their entirety. I watch closely from across the table as she reads her words next to the ones I have written. She is reading quietly, smiles softly, pauses, intentional in her glances as she questions what I wrote. Looking directly at me she tells me, "I'm sure glad I've moved on." She tells me about her contemporary dance and healing from her ballet experiences. She stopped ballet and tells me it has taken nearly 2 years for her toes to heal. Now she is a contemporary dancer and a dance teacher for young children. As a teacher, I wonder how she will teach children what she has learned from her body in relation to ballet practices. Maeve excels in her art experiences of dance and singing. Presently she holds a scholarship for "most promising contemporary" dancer. Watching her dance, I sense her positive spirit and energy. I see Maeve as strong, confident, actively balancing contradictions of what it means to be a girl/woman, a some body who loves to dance. I saw that when I watched her dance in her last spring recital. She choreographed dance works and danced beautifully. I also hear her pleasure as she tells me about teaching children and an upcoming trip to Germany. Maeve tells me, "I never thought this would happen."

## And then some

## Morgan

> I'm glad there's no answers. What can I say, I'm sensing the questions are more important than the answers. I believe that entirely.

Morgan tells me she is shocked at how she talks as she reads what I have written. I think reading her words troubled her, at least a little, for a while. I was not surprised. Morgan's thoughtful responses have pressed me all along to be mindful of my place as a researcher. I am also a friend, and I will not "dumb down" the girls; therefore, I encourage Morgan to edit her talk, clean up her words, cover up grammatical errors, changing the talk to be read. Morgan knows about some of my struggles about writing their stories and showing their photographs. I tell her what troubles my thinking about what research conversations look like. I question whether or not they are really conversations; or are they pseudo-conversations, dialogues, or mono-logues? Whose talking matters? Whose signature in making knowledge claims matters?

Reading the section "Our fathers," Morgan tells me "this is an example of the evaded." In sharing the story with her mother, she finds out that her

father never had any intentions to see her. Her mother tells her she pur-
chased his plane ticket for coming to see her. Morgan said she was ready to
hear the unveiling story of her father: "I don't love what you have written. I
like it." I wonder what stories Morgan will tell about her father in years to
come. What would she tell her children? What photographs will show?

Morgan wants to work as a photographer. She tells me about her "real"
work photographing portfolio work for acting students. She will be attending the arts-based high school for her fifth year just to do her photography.
The school has studio space and camera equipment, which she can continue to use. Morgan talks about pursuing her professional photography career,
perhaps even documenting animals such as cows and horses. Hearing her tell
me that she loves photography is joyous. Being a photographer, an imagemaker, means Morgan remains active in forming, reforming and questioning
aspects of making culture.

**And then some**

**Thya**

Thya is working a summer job in Vancouver. Maeve tells me she is working at a contemporary restaurant and living at Dana's cousins or uncle's
place. I wonder, is Thya seeing Dana? I saw Thya at Maeve's contemporary
spring recital. She was with a different man, although I did not speak with
her. Thya attends the same university as me. She has survived her first year
of arts, and of her winter session, she told Maeve about struggles with her
classes, teachers and classes of "chilly climates": stories of feeling alien. I
sensed her confusion and continue to wonder about the corridors and classes of our university environments, the institutional story of being a first-year
female student. Is there a flicker of experience?

Thya's cameraworks demonstrate how we might respond to girls rather
than constrain girls according to our rigid notions of "good" versus "bad"
behavior. I see Thya's visual narratives as risking to "remove the veil" and
allowing space to frame and reframe prescriptive scripts of being girls. I see
her photographs as destabilizing our assumptions and our normative pre-
scriptions. For Thya, the descriptions of girls' abilities to make sense and
master their bodies undermine adult scripts, which suggest, perhaps, that we
underestimate girls. I see her stories as ones that undermine and call into
question the taken-for-granted in an already interpreted world. Parties, boys
and substance use, seemingly obvious, trouble/problematize what appears
natural, simplistic, or of little consequence.

**And then some**

Hedy

we don't need another hero
we don't need another model
we don't need another ace
we don't need another champion
we don't need another lead
we don't need another heroine
but i
still haven't found what I'm looking for…

Today is Father's Day. I'll give my father a telephone call after he gets home from church. I try to ignore the reality that our clothes dryer is broken and that a laundry pile is rapidly growing. The tool man is unable to repair the dryer until midweek, making a trip to the laundromat inevitable. Housework is a certain reality, for me, as I write through, around and over the artifacts that mark a site of work. I hear my "data-eating" cat whining and howling at our other cat outside my study door. Learning to read pets has been stimulating, particularly my cat who actively seeks outs and chews through photographs. Steve is landscaping our backyard with soil before he builds a new deck. I know he wants me to be finished this dissertation; he has been supportive, more than ever. Our home is 88 years old, and I see it as a works in progress as we strip rooms and floors to their authentic. I like gardening and renovating; for me, this work provides time to think and contemplate. Chloé will be going to her horse back riding lesson. She loves all animals, even magpies. She is presently sitting on my lap getting her morning hug. She asks me "how many pages have you written?" as she reads a few words from the screen and critiques the courier font. I am pulling together the ends of writing up my research, regretting having not used ProCite. I track down my reference list and revise and sift through papers and conference presentations from the past 4 years. I wish it was done. It is like Chloé's math text book of 358 pages. It is not quite done, and it is still hanging on into June. She has had a tough year in her classroom. I can no longer look. We are moving schools. Chloé will attend the same arts-based school that Beth, Morgan and Maeve attended.

I love writing and reading. I think of Dillard (1989), and I imagine books I would like to write. Her words brought comfort on days when I wondered who will teach me to write? "The page, the page, that eternal blankness, the blankness of eternity which you cover slowly, affirming time's scrawl as a right and your daring as necessity" (p. 58). I tell myself I will have a block of time later to write. I have re/presented four girls' multilayered, unfinished, open-ended narratives. These visual narratives are not typical to girls' education, and perhaps, in our composition girls' visual narratives might be seen as a connection of political, theoretical, and symbolic production, the locus of definitions of gender and sexuality, as well as a site of control and desire. Complementing the task of deconstruction is my rewriting of the herstory of girls in terms that firmly locate gender relations as a determining factor in cultural production and signification. Like Bateson (1994), I yearn for double recognition in changing the composition of a life:

> From the point of view of composing a life or managing an institution, the ability to recognize any situation as representing both continuity and change makes it possible to play that double recognition in tune with changing needs, to avoid the changes that reduce flexibility and the constancies that eat away at the necessities of survival. (p. 93)

The necessities for survival mean attending to girls' lived experience, emotionality, and, with them, making sense of what they see. Throughout the cameraworks and listening to stories about their photographs, I see these girls differently. I also see myself differently. Our visual narratives are recreated constructions within an adult-dominated world. I see the girls' cameraworks calling into question the dialectic of reproduction and the resistance to traditional scripts written for girls. I see what they have photographed as a way to turn heads within adult constructions of "normal" and "proper." I see the girls' visual narratives tackling and even mischievously overturning aspects of sex and gender as perceived and purveyed by the dominant culture. But they are doing it by using a delicious and outrageous sense of humor to make sure not only that everybody gets it, but maybe to really give it to them. I see their pictures as a body with a sense of self-actualization, of self-image, of the authority of sexual experience. I also hear the scripted gendered lives influencing compulsory heterosexual relationships and behaviors in fashion, make-up, consumerism, celebrity, glamour and youth culture. I still see our very notions of "good girls" versus "bad girls" lingering: the sign that is stuck with super glue.

The four girls have not been passive recipients of reproduction but rather reflective witnesses, characters, who interact and who resist reconstructed adult definitions for girls. Their visual narratives reveal conflict and pleasure experienced on a daily basis. I have no defensive postures about my research practice; I am not afraid to look and see as I question normative assumptions about authorized knowledge and behavior. I learn about myself with the girls as I think, observe, and listen. I try to imagine alternative, albeit tentative, practices in light of my theoretical reflections. I see the grand narratives that frame and reframe my personal/public life. And naming bodies has meant living with gaps, not papering them over, but actively seeking space to talk about the evaded. I live within and alongside the everyday stories, those rooted in the particular and mundane; on their own, they often uncover and give way to some sort of claim or a universal truth. The cries and whispers prescribed in scripts for marriage, scripts for student, scripts for mothering, scripts for daughters linger in the shadows of my life.

After looking at girls' experiences, what might be learned? What is seen in an already interpreted world and what happens when "we are ready with culturally constructed labels long before we encounter the realities" (Bateson, 1994, p. 4). What happens if we can call our fate by name before we meet? I see the writing/research "on" girls that tell of failing math, of avoiding science, of struggles with self-esteem, of issues of voice and silence, of risk taking behaviors, of pregnancy, and of eating disorders. These stories will not retreat; therefore, I wonder if we are relieved when researchers, teachers, parents, and those in authority name girls' conditions. How might writing/research preserve some diversity? I wonder how these ideologies influence composing other ways to seeing? Are there spaces for girls to look at different stories? I wonder if my work will be read as a possibility that entitles girls to voice and name their stories, conditions and experiences within their lived lives.

We don't need another hero.

The girls are all right.

And my hope for them is to have active lives filled with imagemaking and possibilities to picture a way out, opportunities for making culture by searching and researching. I am not, and neither are the girls in this research, looking for the "victory" narrative, wanting to be rescued or to be another hero. I go to the bookstore and it seems another book concerning girls' lives stares back at me. Journalists, psychologists, reporters and researchers have positioned themselves as writing about girls. I am one of them. As I retell my research experience of the cameraworks, with the girls, I have asked, Will we listen to girls' stories? Will we act on hearing them? Will there be transformation? Will there be change? Will life be different for girls? These are the questions that have dominated my thoughts. I am uncomfortably aware of my position within an institutional community and realize that "narrow" and "distorting" theories flatten the complexities of reality. I have asked myself whether I am speculating without clues? Am I seeing what is not there? I see my interpretations as being in a state of continual flux, unfolding visual narratives, pleat and repleat as I reread and as I see again.

And yet this fall, in September, I will find myself with a class of preservice secondary school teachers. What will I do? What will I say? As I write to what I do not know, I wonder about institutional scripts of being a beginning teacher educator. I see a narrow script for myself. As I reflect on my teacher education experience, I think of my position as researcher, teacher and student and how these experiences inform my coming to know my curricular philosophies. I begin with the assumption that the basis of teacher education is autobiographical. My understanding about teacher education is one of "lifelong and ongoing" (Connelly & Clandinin, 1994) learning. I think about how I will live out and not get hooked up with the "good" teacher educator script. I am awake to what Ellsworth (1989) terms "repressive myths" and believe I am prepared to look at the dilemmas of student "resistance" in relation to a "liberatory" curriculum. I believe it is important to demystify the jargon around critical and liberatory theory in order that prospective teachers consider multiple ways of knowing. Going in search of my questions and in imagining teaching I turn to what Greene (1995) calls "teaching for openings." I think about diverse student experiences in the context of institutional learning:

When we teachers have wanted to believe that education has been a means of giving every living person access to any sort of discourse that person might prefer, when we have wanted to believe that literacy is a personal achievement, a door to personal meaning, it takes an effort for us to realize how deeply literacy is involved in relations of power and how it must be understood in context and in relation to a social world. (p. 110)

I have sat in diverse classes as a student for 33 years. As a learner I found myself reflecting on my reflecting, on my experience, knowing I learned from both educative and miseducative experiences. Often I identify discomfort on my body as an action of efficacy in how I un/learn along the way. As I reflect on the continuum of my teacher education experiences, I have learned and grown from research experiences as a participant and as a researcher in alternative teacher education programs (Bach, Horowitz, & Mickelson, 1996). The last year of my teacher education program was nested in practices of "learning to tell and retell our stories and learning to tell and retell the stories of our students. We do this in our research, in our teaching, in our lives. Telling, retelling and responding to stories is at the heart of our work" (Connelly & Clandinin, 1994, 1995). The practice of telling and retelling stories of my teaching and researching experiences has created discomfort on my body, and only with time and collaborative relationships, I have learned that telling and retelling stories matters.

Throughout my visual narrative inquiry, I have learned that retelling my stories of practice brings about a different understanding of how I see my self as educated, as a knowing body, a body that wants to know. With my ongoing inquiry of becoming a teacher educator, I am mindful to my multiple subjectivities disrupting the living out of my story. As a student with Jean Clandinin I have learned to listen closely. Listening is hard work. As I search to understand my practice of listening and looking, I am awake to my limited position. I have witnessed the embedded practices of teacher as expert and about what matters to the institution.

In my research work with an Alternative Teaching Partnership, I heard administrators say "alternative projects" have a way of "hindering careers" (Bach, Horowitz, & Mickelson, 1995, 1996). In my teaching work, I hear that art matters little in the institution. So I teach marginalized subject matter. I also see how alternative experiences are marginalized within institutions.

On the other hand, I tell stories of myself liking life on the margins.

For me, living on the margins means I can "teach for openings." In my first art methods teaching experience, I was able to build on my personal practical knowledge and the embodied knowing with the visual arts that I have "named" and "historized" within my ongoing professional development. Working with what I know, for example, using a cameraworks experience with students, will build on my commitment that art matters and that visual knowing should be learning.

As a teacher educator, I could never know about all of the student's experiences, oppressions, and understandings of other participants in the class: "This situation makes it impossible for any single voice in the classroom including that of the professor—to assume the position of center or origin of knowledge or authority, of having privileged access to authentic experience or appropriate language" (Ellsworth, 1989, p. 310). As I watch and listen in methods courses for undergraduates and hear teaching stories, I think of Hinchman and Oyler's (1997) experiences of teaching stories in the academy. Like them I am left to wonder about the irony of the "us and them" while teaching within our institutions. A false dichotomy? I imagine my teaching as an ongoing "pedagogical conversation" (Phelan, cited in Hinchman & Oyler, 1997). I wonder about living out the contradictions of teaching in alternative ways, against the grain, knowing inevitable realities of power relations in "rational discourses of reflective teaching paradigms, the being with is split off from the doing. It is the distance from the doing and the being that leaves the preservice teacher free to sit back and reflect" (pp. 7–8). Knowing that the "instrumental student questions" and "professor answers" and "course evaluations" matter, how will I live out what matters to me while encouraging students to find their own curricular philosophies? I wonder if I will have the courage to present myself as a colearner with the students?

I seek to ask, question and actively inquire into the changing meaning and plurality of evaded experiences. I look into the mirror and think about how I draw the veil aside as I look into the predator's eyes. I wonder about the implications of the research: Whose gaze? Whose voice? Whose meaning making? How is this knowledge catalogued in the composition of a teacher education? I trouble and refocus my reading of texts in an already interpreted world. In attempting to pursue "separate visions" (Bateson, 1994, p. 15), I try to understand institutional stories by which we live, and yet questions remain: What am I seeing? What am I looking at? In learning to pursue separate visions I have been pressed to reclaim my gaze. Turning my eyes out to see what matters has meant I have relearned to use my peripheral visions. Beginning my pursuits with Uechi Ryu Karate I am finding my glare. A glare that can "burn through" is a required prowess I am told. This has meant relearning to author my gaze. Learning new skills in a "new" context has been a humbling experience as I learn to connect mind body. I trace back through lived experiences that have been disconnected and miseducative.

In writing stories with images of sur[veil]lance, I acknowledge the discomfort in my body, of seeing texts in the shadows, not merely seeing but looking on those margins of the larger frame that have "generally been kept veiled; but the public ought to be made acquainted with" (Morrison, 1987, p. 110). Will the girls' photographs be seen as defying the conventions and the proprieties of traditional femininity? Or will they be seen as a wish to define themselves according to their own terms, their own pleasures, their own interests, in their own way? It is what I have never seen before that I recognize, images that linger in my mind's i/eye. How can I resist/oppose/deny seeing? I think about images of absent things, and real things themselves, not merely what is seen, but the dialogic tensions, the intention behind the combination of image and text that is narrated. What is learned along the way from sites of discomfort? What comes to light with the veil removed? I think about the pictures that linger and allow for later returns.

Presently, I see a narrow script for a "wanna be" teacher educator, although I imagine multiple ways to disrupt/challenge the fiction of girlhood. What happens when strange images are discarded and denied critical engagement? Perhaps looking and learning from seeing will linger in our research conversations so that new sites might be met with recognition not bewilderment.

The girls' camerawork is exuberant, subversive work in all its richness and variety. I hope their work will add new dimensions to our understanding of the ways that culture shapes school curriculum, our notions of gender and girlhood and thus the ways we see ourselves and others.

an espial
is a detection, disclosure, discovery
so what did you
find
from our showing
did we
strike accord
did we
unearth a different knowing
to see girls as
active and productive
bodies
growing/changing/unfolding

# Appendix A
## Introduction Letter to Parents

Dear Parent(s) of

I would like to take this opportunity to introduce myself and my proposed research to you and your daughter.

My name is Hedy Bach. I completed my Bachelor of Education with a major in Art in 1990 and moved directly into a Masters of Education program, which I completed in the spring of 1993. My Master's work focused on the lives of four girls. Their stories and photographs were the basis of my work entitled *Listening to girls' voices: Narratives of experience*. Currently I am pursuing doctoral studies in the Department of Elementary Education, University of Alberta. My doctoral research will focus on girls' experiences of the evaded curriculum through visual narratives. My study has received ethical approval. I hope to begin collecting data, which will form the basis of my dissertation writing with your daughter.

The research focus of this study is the evaded curriculum, that is, life experiences avoided in the school curriculum in relation to girls' lives in and out of the classroom. The research data will be collected through talking with your daughter, listening to her accounts of her school experiences, and hearing about her interests in photography. Working with your daughter and three other girls I will explore their stories of the evaded curriculum. The eventual purpose of the research is to construct spaces for girls to talk about their experiences. I will work with your daughter outside of the school at a location of her choice (i.e., my home, a mall, a place where they are comfortable). I will negotiate times with your daughter on a biweekly basis over a period of three or more months (no school time will be involved).

All of the girls in this project will be guaranteed anonymity in the final dissertation. I will not at any point in the writing of this dissertation, use your daughter's name, your name(s), or the school name. At the end of this study, the stories and photographs will be shared with the girls.

Should you have any thoughts or concerns regarding this work, I would be delighted to discuss them with you. I am looking forward to working with your daughter.

Sincerely,


Hedy Bach

# Appendix B
## Letter of Parental Consent

Dear Parent(s)

Further to my recent letter regarding my work with your daughter I must seek your written permission to work with and to share your daughter's stories. In order to share her story, I will include parts of your daughter's conversations, anecdotes and photographs in the dissertation. I ask that you sign and return the attached copy of this letter and the enclosed Academic Release Form in order to permit me to begin work with and to share your daughter's story.

In the future, when speaking or writing of our work together I will at no time reveal the name of the school, your name(s), or your daughter's name. I will be careful about making sure confidential information about your daughter is protected. As discussed, please remember that I will be sharing with your daughter the photographs and stories that will be used in the dissertation. Eventually I will also share these stories and visual representations with other people as a part of research presentations.

I am also aware that, as parents, some of your story will be shared through your daughter's stories/photographs. Therefore, as indicated in the Academic Release Form, because I feel it is important that parents know and understand my involvement with their daughters I will be pleased to discuss the project with you. Your daughter is free to withdraw from the project at any time.

Should you have concerns at any time regarding this work, please contact me at (wk) 492–7770. Thank you for providing me with this opportunity to work with your daughter.

Sincerely,


Hedy Bach


I grant permission for_____
to participate in the project: a visual narrative concerning curriculum, girls, photography etc.


Signed: _____
Date: _____

# Appendix C
## Academic Release Form

Hedy Bach, Doctoral Student * University of Alberta * CRTED * Education
South * Edmonton, AB. * 403-492-7770 * fax 403-492-0236
* hedybach@ualberta.ca
*************************************************************************************
My signature below indicates my permission for Hedy Bach to
keep/make professional use of:

( ) Photographs ( ) Audio Tape Recordings

I understand that this Release Form indicates my permission for the
above to be viewed by other people for educational or for teaching purposes
and others related to this work, including the girls, participants in work-
shops, conferences, lectures, and classes led by Hedy Bach, and/or in professional publications authored by her for reading by other educators. I understand that this does NOT include access by the general public except as participants in the above. I understand that Hedy Bach will at all times respect
the professional ethics and confidential nature required by such a Release.

I understand that should she seek a wider audience for material that
might in any way disclose my identity, she will either sufficiently disguise
such details so as to prevent my recognition, or she will have to get specific
extended permission from me in writing before that time to use any of it. I
agree to keep her informed of my current address for such purposes.

If this more public use is already acceptable to me, I have indicated such wider general public access/academic/scholarly permission below. I understand that I may revoke any or all Releases on file with her at any time by sending her a written notice of revocation by Registered mail. I agree that any other method of revocation will not be legally binding upon her.

Therefore, in return for copies of these photos, I hereby agree to her full use of material indicated in the above checklist, for professionals-only audiences, with any particular restrictions indicated immediately below.

Restrictions (if any):_____

Name (print):_____

Address:_____

Phone:_____Date:_____

(signature): _____

\*\*\*\*\*\*\*\*\*\*\*\*\*\*\*\*\*\*\*\*\*\*\*\*\*\*\*\*\*\*\*\*\*\*\*\*\*\*\*\*\*\*\*\*\*\*\*\*\*\*\*\*\*\*\*\*\*\*\*\*\*\*\*\*\*\*\*\*\*\*\*\*\*\*\*\*\*\*\*

I give Hedy Bach permission to use these photos, photo-documents, and anecdotes in academic (books, journal articles, video etc.) that CAN be seen by the general public. (Please check one):

* YES, without any conditions ( )
* YES, but with the conditions listed below ( )
* Not now, but contact me later for possibility for certain specific situations ( )
* Not at all, ever ( )

Name (print):_____Date:_____

Witness to the above signature(s) for person underage:

(signature(s):_____

# Bibliography

Ackerman, D. (1990). *A natural history of the senses*. New York: Vintage.

Aisenberg, N., & Harrington, M. (1988). *Women of academe: Outsiders in the sacred grove*. Amherst: The University of Massachusetts Press.

Alcoff, L. (1991). The problem of speaking for others. *Cultural Critique, 5*(1), 5–32.

Alcoff, L., & Gray, L. (1993). Survivor discourse: Transgression or recuperation? *Signs, 18*(2), 260–290.

American Association of University Women Educational Foundation. (1992). *How schools shortchange girls*. Washington, DC: AAUW and National Education Association.

Amos, T. (1991). Crucify. On *Little earthquakes* [CD]. Scarborough: Warner Music.

Amos, T. (1994). Cornflake girl. On *Under the pink* [CD]. Scarborough: Warner Music.

Arbus, D. (1972) *Diane Arbus*. New York: An Aperture Monograph.

Bach, H. (1993). *Listening to girls' voices: Narratives of experience.* Unpublished master's thesis, University of Alberta, Edmonton, Alberta, Canada.

Bach, H. (1995). Listening to girls' voices: If not now, when? *Teaching Education, 7*(1), 109–116.

Bach, H. (1996a, April). *Troubling photography.* A roundtable session presented at the annual meeting of the American Educational Research Association Invisible College, New York.

Bach, H. (1996b, April). *Visual narratives: Girls dancing with the evaded curriculum.* A roundtable session presented at the annual meeting of the American Educational Research Association, New York.

Bach, H. (1996c, April). *Visual narratives: Not a basic photograph.* Poster session presented at the annual meeting of the American Educational Research Association, New York.

Bach, H. (1996d, January). *Visual narratives: Viewing the evaded curriculum.* Multi-media paper presented at the annual meeting of the Conference on Qualitative Research in Education, University of Georgia, Athens.

Bach, H. (1996e, June). *Schoolgirls: Visual narratives of the evaded curriculum.* Poster session presented at the annual meeting of the Canadian Society for the Study of Education, Brock University, St. Catherines, ON.

Bach, H. (1997a). Seen any good movies? Creating space to talk about popular culture. *Canadian Social Studies, 31*(2), 87–89.

Bach, H. (1997b, March). *Visual narratives: Contests of meaning.* Paper presented at the annual meeting of the International Conference on Teacher Research, Louis University, Evanston.

Bach, H. (1997c, March). *Visual narratives: Photography as research.* Invited address presented at the annual meeting of the American Educational Research Association, Chicago.

Bach, H., Clandinin, D. J., & Greggs, R. (1992, October). *Hearing the voices of young girls.* Paper presented at the meeting of the American Association of University Women/Mills College Conference, Oakland.

Bach, H., Horowitz, M., & Mickelson, J. R. (1995). *Teaching partnerships: The pace and space of diversity.* Edmonton, Alberta: University of Alberta, Centre for Research for Teacher Education and Development.

Bach, H., Horowitz, M., & Mickelson, J. R. (1996, June). *So you want to be a teacher educator: Who do we learn from?* Paper presented at the annual meeting of the Canadian Society for the Study of Education, Brock University, St. Catherines.

Bach, H., Kennedy, M., & Mickelson, J. R. (1997, March). *Bodies at work: Sensory knowing.* Paper presented at the annual meeting of the American Educational Research Association, Chicago.

Barthes, R. (1981). *Camera lucida.* New York: Hill and Wang.

Bateson, M. C. (1994). *Peripheral visions.* New York: Harper Collins.

Becker, H. (1974). Photography and sociology. *Studies in the Anthropology of Visual Communication, 1*(1) 3–26.

Becker, H. (1981). *Exploring society photographically.* Chicago: University of Chicago Press.

Belenky, M., Clinchy, M., Goldberger, R., & Tarule, J. (1986). *Women's ways of knowing: The development of self, voice, and mind.* New York: Basic.

Berger, J. (1972). *Ways of seeing.* London: Penguin.

Berger, J. (1980). *About looking.* London: Writer and Readers Publishing.

Berger, J., & Mohr, J. (1982). *Another way of telling.* New York: Pantheon.

Blake, W. (1981). *The color book.* New York: Watson-Guptill Publications.

Bolton, R. (1989). *The contest of meaning: Critical histories of meaning.* Cambridge, MA: MIT Press.

Bordo, S. (1991). Material girl: The effacement of postmodern culture. In L. Goldstein (Ed.), *The female body: Figures, styles, speculations* (pp. 106–131). Ann Arbor: The University Press of Michigan Press.

234

Brettle, J., & Rice, S. (1994). *Private bodies—private states: New views on photography, representation and gender.* New York: Manchester University Press.

Brown, L. M., & Gilligan, C. (1992). *Meeting at the crossroads: Women's psychology and girls' development.* Cambridge, MA: Harvard University Press.

Brownmiller, S. (1986). *Femininity.* London: Paladin.

Calkins, L. (1991). *Living between the lines.* Toronto: Irwin Publishing.

Casey, K. (1995). The new narrative research in education. In M. Apple (Ed.), *Review of research in education* (Vol. 21, pp. 211–254). Washington, DC: American Educational Research Association.

Cixous, H. (1994). *The Hélène Cixous reader* (S. Sellers, Ed.). London: Routledge.

Clandinin, D. J., & Connelly, F. M. (1994). Personal experience methods. In N. Denzin & Y. Lincoln (Eds.), *Handbook for qualitative research* (pp. 413–427). San Francisco: Sage.

Clandinin, D. J., Davies, A., Hogan, P., & Kennard, B. (1993). *Learning to teach, teaching to learn: Stories of collaboration in teacher education.* New York: Teachers College Press.

Code, L. (1987). *Epistemic responsibility.* London: University Press of New England.

Code, L. (1991). *What can she know?: Feminist theory and the construction of knowledge.* London: Cornell University Press.

Code, L. (1992). Persons and others. In D. Shogan (Ed.), *A reader in feminist ethics* (pp. 89–106). Toronto: Canadian Scholars' Press.

Collier, J., & Collier, M. (1986). *Visual anthropology: Photography as a research method.* Albuquerque: University of New Mexico Press.

Connelly, F. M., & Clandinin, D. J. (1988). *Teachers as curriculum planners: Narratives of experience.* New York: Teachers College Press.

Connelly, F. M., & Clandinin, D. J. (1990). Stories of experience and narrative inquiry. *Educational Researcher, 19*(5), 2–14.

Connelly, F. M., & Clandinin, D. J. (1994). Telling teaching stories. *Teacher Education Quarterly, 21*(1), 145–158.

Connelly, F. M., & Clandinin, D. J. (1995). *Teacher's professional knowledge landscapes.* New York: Teachers College Press.

Derrida, J. (1981). *Positions.* Chicago: University of Chicago Press.

Dewey, J. (1904). The relation of theory to practice in education. In *National Society for the Scientific Study of Education* (pp. 9–30). Bloomington: Public School Publishing.

Dewey, J. (1938). *Experience & education.* New York: Collier.

Dillard, A. (1989). *The writing life.* New York. Harper Perennial.

Ellsworth, E. (1989). Why doesn't this feel empowering? Working through the repressive myths of critical pedagogy. *Harvard Educational Review, 59*(3), 297–324.

Engerer, A., & Wuohela, L. (1997). *The glass/architecture project: Parting the veil.* Toronto: Goethe-Institute.

English, F. (1988). The utility of the camera in qualitative inquiry. *Educational Researcher, 17*(4), 8–15.

Ewing, W. (1994). *The body: Photographs of the human form.* San Francisco: Chronicle Books.

Fine, M. (1994a). Dis-stance and other stances: Negotiations of power inside feminist research. In A. Gitlin (Ed.), *Power and method* (pp. 13–35). New York: Routledge.

Fine, M. (1994b). Working the hyphens: Reinventing self and other in qualitative research. In N. Denzin & Y. Lincoln (Eds.), *Handbook for qualitative research* (pp. 70–82). San Francisco: Sage.

Fine, M., & Macpherson, P. (1995, April). *Hungry for an us.* Paper presented at the annual meeting of the American Educational Research Association, San Francisco, CA.

Fine, M., & Zane, N. (1991). Bein' wrapped too tight: When low income women drop out of school. *Women's Studies Quarterly, 19*(2), 77–99.

Fraser, N. (1989). *Unruly practices: Power, discourse and gender in contemporary social theory.* Minneapolis: University of Minnesota.

Gaskell, J., & McLaren, A. (1987). *Women and education: A Canadian perspective.* Calgary: Detselig Enterprises Limited.

Gaskell, J., McLaren, A., & Novogrodsky, M. (1989). *Claiming an education: Feminism and Canadian schools.* Toronto: Our Schools/Our selves Educational Foundation.

Gilligan, C. (1982). *In a different voice.* Cambridge: Harvard University Press.

Gilligan, C. (1987). Adolescent development reconsidered. *Adolescent Social Behavior and Health, 37*(Fall), 63–92.

Gilligan, C. (1991). Joining the resistance: Psychology, politics, girls and women. In L. Goldstein (Ed.), *The female body: Figures, styles, speculations* (pp. 12–47). Ann Arbor: The University of Michigan Press.

Gilligan, C., Lyons, N., & Hanmer, T. (1990). *Making connections: The relational worlds of adolescent girls at Emma Willard school.* Cambridge, MA: Harvard University Press.

Gold, S. (1989). Ethical issues in visual field work. In G. Blank, J. McCartney, & E. Brent (Eds.), *New technology in sociology: Practical applications in research and work* (pp. 99–109). New Jersey: Transaction Publishers.

Greene, M. (1991). Blue guitars and the search for curriculum. In G. Willis & W. Schubert (Eds.), *Reflections from the heart of educational inquiry: Understanding curriculum and teaching through the arts* (pp. 107–122). Albany: State University of New York Press.

Greene, M. (1993). Reflections on postmodernism and education. *Educational Policy, 7*(2), 206–211.

Greene, M. (1995). *Releasing the imagination: Essays on education, the arts, and social change.* San Francisco: Jossey-Bass.

Grimm, B. (1959). *Favourite tales from Grimm and Anderson.* Prague: Bedford Press.

Grumet, M. (1988). *Bitter milk: Women and teaching.* Amherst: University of Massachusetts Press.

Gunderloy, M., & Janice, C.G. (1992). *The world of zines.* New York: Penguin.

Haacke, H. (1975). *Framing and being framed.* Halifax: Press of the Nova Scotia College of Art and Design.

Harding, S. (1986). *The question of science in feminism.* Ithaca: Cornell University Press.

Harper, D. (1987). The visual ethnographic narrative. *Visual Anthropology, 1*(1), 1–19.

Harper, D. (1989). Visual sociology: Expanding sociological vision. In G. Blank, J. McCartney, & E. Brent (Eds.), *New technology in sociology: Practical applications in research and work* (pp. 81–98). New Jersey: Transaction Publishers.

Hartman, J., & Messer-Daidow, E. (1991). *(En)gendering knowledge: Feminists in academe.* Knoxville: University of Tennessee Press.

Haug, F. (1987). *Female sexualization: A collective work of memory.* London: Verso.

Hebdige, D. (1988). *Hiding in the light.* London: A Comedia book published by Routledge.

Heilbrun, C. (1988). *Writing a woman's life.* New York: Ballantine Books.

Herron, L., & Williams, V. (1996). *Illuminations: Women writing on photography from the 1850s to the present.* Durham: Duke University Press.

Hinchman, K., & Oyler, C. (1997, March). *Us and them: Finding irony in our teaching methods.* Paper presented at the annual meeting of the American Educational Research Association, Chicago.

Holmes, J., & Silverman, E. (1992). *We're here listen to us.* Ottawa: Canadian Advisory Council on the Status of Women.

hooks, b. (1984). *Feminist theory: From margin to center.* Boston: South End Press.

hooks, b. (1989). *Talking back: Thinking feminist, thinking black.* Boston: South End Press.

hooks, b. (1994). *Teaching to transgress: Education as the practice of freedom.* New York: Routledge.

hooks, b. (1995). *Art on my mind: Visual politics.* New York: The New Press.

Jaggar, A., & Bordo, S. (1992). *Gender/body/knowledge: Feminist reconstructions of being and knowing.* New Jersey: Rutgers University Press.

Johnson, M. (1987). *The body in the mind: Bodily basis of imagination, reason, and meaning.* Chicago: University of Chicago Press.

Keller, E.F. (1985). *Reflections on gender and science.* New Haven: Yale University Press.

Krieger, S. (1991). *Social science and the self: Personal essays on an art form.* New Brunswick, N. J.: Rutgers University Press.

Kristeva, J. (1986). *The Kristeva reader* (Toril Moi, Ed.). Oxford: Basil Blackwell.

Le Dœuff, M. (1991). *Hipparachia's choice: An essay concerning women, philosophy, etc.* Cambridge: Blackwell.

Leland, N. (1990). *The creative artist.* Cincinnati: North Light Books.

Lessing, D. (1962). *The golden notebook*. London: Michael Joseph.

Lingis, A. (1994). *Foreign bodies*. New York: Routledge.

Lorde, A. (1984). *Sister outsider: Essays and speeches*. New York: The Crossing Press.

MacGregor, D. (1997, February, 22). Dr. Sacks stalks the strange. *The Globe and Mail*, D16.

MacIntosh, P. (1992). *How schools shortchange girls*. Washington, DC: AAUW and National Education Association.

Martin, R., & Spence, J. (1989). New portraits for old: The use of the camera in therapy. In R. Betterton (Ed.), *Looking on images of femininity in the visual arts and media* (pp. 104–118). London: Pandora.

May, W. (1977). Code and covenant or philanthropy and contract? In J. Stanley, A.J. Dyck, & W. Curran (Eds.), *Ethics in medicine: Historical perspective and contemporary concerns* (pp. 65–76). Cambridge: MIT.

May, W. (1980). Doing ethics: The bearing of ethical theories on field-work. *Social Problems, 27*, 358–370.

Miller, A. (1984). *Thou shalt not be aware: Society's betrayal of the child*. New York: Farrar, Straus and Giroux.

Miller, A. (1990). *For your own good: Hidden cruelty in child-rearing and the roots of violence*. New York: Noonday.

Mitchell, W. (1992). *The reconfigured eye: Visual truth in the post-photographic era*. Cambridge: The MIT Press.

Morrison, T. (1987). The site of memory. In W. Zinsser (Ed.), *Inventing the truth* (pp. 101–124). Boston: Houghton Mifflin.

Noddings, N. (1984). *Caring: A feminine approach to ethics and moral education*. London: University of California Press.

Noddings, N. (1986). Fidelity in teaching, teacher education, and research for teaching. *Harvard Educational Review, 56*(1), 496–510.

Orenstein, P. (1994). *Schoolgirls: Young women, self esteem, and the confidence gap*. New York: Doubleday.

Owens, C. (1994). *Beyond recognition: Representation, power, and culture*. Berkeley: University of California Press.

Paley, N. (1995). *Finding art's place: Experiments in contemporary education and culture*. New York: Routledge.

Pinar, W. (1976). *Toward a poor curriculum*. Dubuque: Kendall/Hunt Publishing.

Pipher, M. (1994). *Reviving Ophelia: Saving the selves of adolescent girls*. New York: Ballantine Books.

Pollock, G. (1988). *Vision and difference: Femininity, feminism and histories of art*. New York: Routledge.

Rich, A. (1979). *On lies, secrets, and silence: Selected Prose 1966–1978*. New York: W.W. Norton.

Rich, A. (1993). *What is found there: Notebooks on poetry and politics*. New York: W.W. Norton.

Roland Martin, J. (1982). Excluding women from the educational realm. *Harvard Educational Review, 52*(2), 133–148.

Roland Martin, J. (1986). Redefining the educated person: Rethinking the significance of gender [Special Issue]. *Educational Researcher, June/July*, 6–10.

Rosenau, P. (1992). *Post-modernism and the social sciences: Insights, inroads, and intrusions*. Princeton: Princeton University Press.

Rosler, M. (1989a). In, around, and afterthoughts (on documentary photography). In R. Bolton (Ed.), *The contest of meaning* (pp. 303–286). Cambridge: MIT Press.

Rosler, M. (1989b). Teaching photography: A critical issue. *The New Art Examiner, 9*(4), 35.

Rubin, N. (1994). *Ask me if I care*. Berkeley: Ten Speed Press.

Ruddick, S. (1989). *Maternal thinking: Toward a politics of peace*. Boston: Beacon Press.

Sacks, O. (1997). *The island of the color blind*. New York: Alfred Knopf.

Sadker, M., & Sadker, D. (1980). Sexism in teacher education. *Harvard Educational Review, 50*(1), 36–46.

Sadker, M., & Sadker, D. (1994). *Failing at fairness: How America's schools cheat girls*. New York: Charles Scribner's Sons.

Salinger, A. (1995). *In my bedroom: Teenagers in their bedrooms*. San Francisco: Chronicle Books.

Solomon, E. (1996, April). Great ball of fire: Tori Amos blows her top at men, women and god. *Shift*, 34–38.

Sontag, S. (1966). *Against interpretation*. New York: Farrar, Straus and Giroux.

Sontag, S. (1977). *On photography*. New York: Farrar, Straus and Giroux.

Spence, J. (1986). *Putting myself in the picture*. London: Camden Press.

Spence, J. (1995). *Cultural sniping: The art of transgression*. London: Routledge.

Stein, G. (1926). *Composition as explanation*. London: Hogarth Press.

Style, E. (1992). *How schools shortchange girls*. Washington DC: AAUW and National Education Association.

Style, E. (1993). *Keynote address*. Presented at American Association of University Women/Mills College Conference. Conference proceedings. Oakland.

Suleiman, S. (1994). *Risking who one is: Encounters with contemporary art and literature*. Cambridge: Harvard University Press.

242

Trinh, Minh-Ha, T. (1989). *Woman' native' other*. Bloomington: Indiana University Press.

Tucker, M. (1994). *Bad girls*. New York: The New Museum of Contemporary Art.

Walkerdine, V. (1989). Femininity as performance. *Oxford Review of Education, 15*(3), 267–279.

Walkerdine, V. (1990). *Schoolgirl fictions*. London: Verso.

Weedon, C. (1987). *Feminist practice and poststructuralist theory*. New York: Basil Blackball.

Weiser, J. (1975). PhotoTherapy: Photography as a verb. *PhotoTherapy, 4*(2), 33–36.

Weiser, J. (1993). *Phototherapy techniques: Exploring the secrets of personal snapshots and family albums*. San Francisco: Jossey-Bass.

Wittig, M. (1992). *The straight mind and other essays*. Boston: Beacon Press.

Wolf, N. (1990). *The beauty myth*. Toronto: Random House.

Wollstonecraft, M. (1792). *Vindication of the rights of a woman*. London: Penguin.

Woolf, V. (1929). *A room of one's own*. New York: Harcourt, Brace and World.

Ziller, R. (1990). *Photographing the self: Methods for observing personal orientations*. Newbury Park: Sage.

Zimmerman, D. (1991). Seeing, reading, knowing: The lesbian appropriation of literature. In J. Hartman & E. Messer-Daidow (Eds.), *(En)gendering knowledge: Feminists in academe* (pp. 85–99). Knoxville: University of Tennessee Press.

# Index